JANE AUSTEN TODAY

JANE AUSTEN TODAY

EDITED BY

JOEL WEINSHEIMER

THE UNIVERSITY OF GEORGIA PRESS

ATHENS

Library of Congress Catalog Card Number: 75-11447
International Standard Book Number: 0-8203-0382-8

The University of Georgia Press, Athens 30602

Printed in the United States of America

CONTENTS

PREFACE

It can never be surprising that an author of novels, popular or otherwise, should slip into oblivion, there to be disturbed only by the occasional featherduster of an antiquarian. Attrition among novelists is especially high, since the novel (unlike drama) is a genre peculiarly seductive to the unserious writer. A frequenter of the streets rather than the springs of Helicon, the muse of the novel seems available to all, with short and informal wooing. But since fiction is so often attempted and mediocrity so widely achieved, excellence is therefore the less accessible. The novel is perhaps the least likely genre by which an author can hope to endure.

Jane Austen, however, has endured, as this volume attests. Never has respect for her accomplishments been higher or the reasons for it more thoroughly documented than during this bicentenary year. Her novels are not known as meticulously preserved curiosities in the rare book room; instead, they are dog-eared paperbacks lying on the desks and armchairs of a dozen nations. Now, two hundred years after her birth, Jane Austen is read, and no more substantial praise is possible.

Adulation, of course, is a sure sign of moribundity, both in author and reader. But the original essays here collected participate in the continuing dialectical renewal of Jane Austen which is professional criticism's distinctive form of praise. Chosen for their diversity in reputation, critical methodology, and literary specialization, the contributors nevertheless share the esteem for Jane Austen that comes from close scrutiny of each of her novels.

Yet the bicentennial appeared to me an occasion calling for broader speculations than those possible in readings of single works; hence I invited only general and judicial appraisals. This focus seemed particularly appropriate because, despite the considerable upsurge of interest in Jane Austen during the last twenty years, the growth of her reputation has been hindered by charges that she is "limited." For those who respond to these charges, more is at stake than pushing Austen stock in some bogus literary market. What we discover in her novels is largely a function of what we seek and are willing to find there; our expectations are guided by our judgment of her worth. This collection, then, directly confronts the fundamental problem of assessing Jane Austen's achievement—a process that requires an examination of both the novels themselves and the methods of interpretation and evaluation we apply to them. The advantage of so focusing the contributions is that they have become reciprocally suggestive—sometimes by way of supplement, sometimes rebuttal—and I have arranged them so as to clarify their interconnections. Thus although the collection cannot claim the coherence of a book by a single author, nevertheless a reader who finds one essay specially appealing may find the next equally so and will by degrees, I venture to predict, discover he has read them all.

All quotations from Jane Austen's novels and letters are from *The Novels of Jane Austen: The Text Based on Collation of the Early Editions*, ed. R. W. Chapman, 3rd ed. (London: Oxford University Press, 1932-1934), 5 vols., and *Jane Austen's Letters to her Sister Cassandra and Others*, ed. R. W. Chapman, 2nd ed. (London: Oxford University Press, 1952). Page references to both novels and letters are included parenthetically in the text.

Professors Greene, McMaster and Weinsheimer presented oral versions of their essays at the University of Victoria's Jane Austen Bicentenary Commemoration, ably directed by Professor Samuel Macey, in April 1975.

JANE AUSTEN TODAY

ALISTAIR M. DUCKWORTH

PROSPECTS AND RETROSPECTS

> The ultimate goal of the hermeneutic process is to understand an author better than he understood himself.
>
> Wilhelm Dilthey

> The problems of style can only be treated by reference to what I shall refer to as the "layeredness" (*feuilleté*) of the discourse. . . . If up until now we have looked at the text as a species of fruit with a kernel (an apricot, for example), the flesh being the form and the pit being the content, it would be better to see it as an onion, a construction of layers (or levels, or systems) whose body contains, finally, no heart, no kernel, no secret, no irreducible principle, nothing except the infinity of its own envelopes—which envelop nothing other than the unity of its own surfaces.
>
> Roland Barthes

I

In spite of a staggering amount of critical attention Jane Austen can hardly be said, in her bicentennial year, to be understood better than she understood herself.[1] Skeptics could argue that no common agreement has been reached on the most basic questions. Is her morality grounded in a deeply religious view of life, or is it secular and Aristotelian in nature? How far is it limited, in either instance, by being "ideological," the veiled expression of class interests? Is her irony rhetorically directed at moral and social abuses, or secretly critical of the standards it seems to uphold, or a neutral mode whereby Jane Austen comes to terms with a contradictory world? If little agreement has been reached on such general questions, it can hardly be said to exist, either, on the interpretation of single works. Of the six novels three—*Sense and Sensibility*, *Mansfield Park*, and *Persuasion*—remain problem novels, and of the seven heroines two—Marianne Dashwood and Fanny Price—resist all appeals to interpretive consensus. There would seem to be good reason for accepting Roland Barthes's insistence on the plural significance of literary texts and his criticism of academic attempts to discover kernels of meaning at the heart of novels.

Certainly much Austen criticism has assumed, however unselfconsciously, the hermeneutic goal of a valid understanding of her novels through the imaginative recovery of the language and attitudes she shared with her culture. But modern skepticism as to the possibility of possessing past meanings, along with new insistences on the "symbolic," or "enigmatic," or "constitutively ambiguous" nature of literary language, has put in doubt objective interpretation through historical reconstruction, or, for that matter, through any interpretive means. For the student of Barthes the lack of agreement among Austen critics, after allowance has been made for error and eccentricity, might be taken as proof of the polysemous nature even of "classic" literature. Though her novels are, in his terms, *lisible* rather than *scriptible*—limited, that is, in the plurality of their significances rather than, as in the posited instance of the ideal modern text, infinitely open to the composition of meaning by the reader—they are exceedingly complex structures, made up of networks or codes that resist the discovery of single keys and properly invite a large number of "constructed" readings. To assume otherwise by seeking determinate readings is to be critically naive, guilty of *asymbolie*, the sin of Raymond Picard. To recognize, on the other hand, that Jane Austen's novels transcend the tendency of "classic" texts to put constraints on meaning may be the way to true critical sophistication and to the liberation—of the author as well as the reader—from ideological bad faith.[2]

This will not be, however, the proposal of this essay. I do not think it probable that *la nouvelle critique*, in validating plurality as an interpretive principle, can resolve scholarly and critical disagreement over the meaning of Jane Austen's novels. Nor do I concede that historical scholarship, in seeking the recovery of contemporary meanings, has pursued a mistaken and fruitless direction. As interpreter, I can hardly claim to meet Jane Austen as an equal, "dans la même condition difficile, face au même objet: le langage" (*Critique et Verité*, p. 47). And I cannot accept the implication in Barthes, noted by Frank Kermode, that the "only hope for *lisible* texts is that they allow themselves, in limited ways, to be treated as modern."[3] Least of all, if I discover at the "heart" of Jane Austen's novels posited "origins" for moral behavior, in religion or in received moral wisdom, do I consider that this brands her—or me—as "ideological," and hence loathsome.

What I do propose is that the views of Barthes on literary form and style stand as an energizing challenge to Austen criticism, as well as to the criticism of fiction generally. His insistence on the diminished—not to say vanished—authority of the author and of the text considered as a historical object, as well as his valuation of the critic who stands equal with the creative writer in the "production" of meaning, has already found support or response from a number of unlikely quarters. When E. D. Hirsch, Jr., perhaps the major American apologist for the validity of objective interpretation, can concede, in asserting "the ontological equality of all interpreted meanings," that "we, not our texts, are the makers of the meanings we understand, a text being only an occasion for meaning, in itself an ambiguous form devoid of the consciousness where meaning abides," we can sense which way the wind is blowing.[4]

So far, however, Austen criticism has remained largely unaffected by such breezes from France. Critics have generally assumed, even in the face of radically different interpretations, a confident ability to discover objective meanings. Typically such criticism has not been theoretically self-conscious. There have been some Marxist interpretations (Arnold Kettle, Raymond Williams) and some psychologizing (Edmund Wilson, D. W. Harding, Geoffrey Gorer, Marvin Mudrick), but the bulk of academic criticism has stayed within traditional corridors: we have had sound scholarly studies and good analyses of a New Critical (Reuben Brower), or neo-Aristotelian (Wayne Booth), or English commonsensical (Malcolm Bradbury, W. J. Harvey) kind.[5] I certainly intend no dismissal of these contributions, and must acknowledge that no category of Jane Austen's genius has received more intensive treatment, especially in recent years, than her style.

Every appreciative critic from Sir Walter Scott onwards, of course, has had something to say about Jane Austen's style, and even when she has been depreciated, for example by Charlotte Brontë and H. W. Garrod, stylistic criteria have been invoked. From the outset of modern Austen studies, moreover, R. W. Chapman stood as a proprietary sentinel at the gates of good usage, and critics like Lascelles (1939), Wright (1953), and Babb (1962) have since insisted on evaluating her art and moral vision through careful stylistic analysis. The studies of Ten Harmsel (1964), Bradbrook (1966), and Moler (1968) were primarily investigations into the literary and philosophic backgrounds of her work, but they have nevertheless lent support to F. R. Leavis's partly stylistic claim, made in *The Great Tradition* (1947), that Jane Austen in her indebtedness to others provides an illuminating study of individual originality in relation to tradition. On top of all this, no fewer than five studies have recently appeared in as many years, all concerned with Jane Austen's style.[6]

It is not my intention to summarize what these studies have said on such topics as Jane Austen's vocabulary, syntax, symbolism, and her use of the free indirect style. It will be sufficient here to affirm that, despite some duplicated effort, especially on the subject of Jane Austen's words, these works are a substantial contribution to Austen studies. Their collective insistence is on the need for an extremely close attention to her style, for all agree that Jane Austen is among the most linguistically self-conscious of authors. With this in mind, I shall examine the methods of two of these studies in some detail and then look at what is perhaps the most interesting essay to appear on a single novel in the last decade. As I do this, I shall have in mind the situation of critical disarray described at the beginning, and I shall be hearing at my back the hypothetical claims of the structuralist approach.

II

K. C. Phillipps's excellent *Jane Austen's English* can best be viewed as a thorough extension of R. W. Chapman's appendices on vocabulary and grammar added to his edition of *Sense and Sensibility*. To say that it might equally well take its place next to Fowler's *Modern English Usage* on the library shelf as in the Jane Austen section is to pay tribute to its fascination as well as to suggest its interpretive limitations. It is not intended as a critical work—indeed when it picks up controversial issues in stylistic criticism it tends to drop them like hot cakes.[7] What follows, then, is not to be thought of as a criticism of the study but as a line of thought arising from it.

Briefly, Phillipps argues that Jane Austen's English has to be understood on its own lexical, syntactic and grammatical terms, that it is different, often in very subtle ways, from the English of the seventeenth and early eighteenth centuries as well as from modern English, and that by understanding how it differs from earlier and later usage we can understand her meanings and see in what ways she has endorsed her favored, and negatively labelled her imperfect, characters. That Jane Austen has her deficient characters use substandard English is hardly new and not claimed as such; what validates the study is the wealth of its detail and the comprehensiveness of its treatment.

Yet this very comprehensiveness is likely to raise questions. Naturally, selection of some kind is necessary. Phillipps's principle of selection is that of a historical or socio-linguistic grammarian rather than that of a literary critic, and the usefulness of his study to literary criticism is less than might be thought at first. In spite of his attention to a huge number of Jane Austen's words (more than five hundred are indexed), Austen critics are likely to miss words they consider important: I would like to know what Phillipps has to say about such words as *business*, *bustle*, *profession*, recurrent key terms in her novels. There is as yet no concordance to her works, and even if there were, its critical use, too, might be limited; as David Lodge has rightly insisted, for the literary critic "the significance of repetition is not to be determined statistically" (*Language of Fiction*, p. 85). Curiously, the word that Lodge considers of prime importance in his reading of *Mansfield Park*, *judgment*, is not discussed by Phillipps.

One point to be made here concerns where we are to locate norms of usage in Jane Austen. Phillipps claims that vulgar speakers in her novels–Lucy Steele, Mrs. Jennings–use expressions that were once acceptable, for example in the correspondence of the Verney ladies, but had become substandard usage by Jane Austen's time as a result of the work of such grammarians as Robert Lowth and Lindley Murray. The argument is an interesting one in terms of a history of English usage, but it is less relevant to an interpretation of Jane Austen's novels. The grammatical standards by which we judge Lucy Steele, or Mrs. Jennings, or Harriet Smith, or Mr. Collins, are internal rather than external, deviations from the norms that the texts set up and lead us to accept. When Lydia Bennet writes to Harriet Forster gleefully describing her elopement with Wickham (*PP*, 291-292) she may write substandard English of this kind that was acceptable in genteel female correspondence of the seventeenth and early eighteenth centuries; but the standard by which she is to be judged is the spoken and written English of her elder sister Elizabeth, or the language of the novel's narrator, and not the English usage prescribed by contemporary grammarians. Lydia's limping compound sentences, her substitution of *who* where *whom* is required, the too frequent appearance of *I*, are all in marked contrast both to the vitality, grammatical subordination and verbal wit of Elizabeth's conversation and to the more somber, Johnsonian style of her letters following the news of Lydia's disgrace.

Moreover, as soon as we turn to specific examples of substandard usage in the novels we are likely to find that such usage is only one of a number of negative indications of character. In the passage cited, for example, Lydia's immorality or "insubordination" is not only marked by her syntactical looseness, solecisms, and lexical exaggeration; it is also revealed by her immoderate mirth ("What a good joke it will be! I can hardly write for laughing.") Lydia's tendency to laughter, like her habits of running everywhere and speaking loudly and rudely at inappropriate times, marks her morally unrestrained conduct. In all these areas she may be evaluated against her sister's more disciplined moral behavior. But Lydia serves not only as a degraded version of Elizabeth; she is, after all, Elizabeth's sister; and genetically or thematically, and in any case linguistically, Elizabeth has something of Lydia in her. She, too, dearly loves a laugh, is often described as running, and, as Lady Catherine learns at Rosings, can give her opinion very decidedly for so young a person. Her behavior, then, can be rated by comparison with Lydia's, though we should observe that the comparison involves multiple terms and is not simply a matter of the quality of the English spoken or written. The result is, of course, always in Elizabeth's favor. It is right that whims and inconsistencies should divert her, that she should run up to Jane's bedroom when Jane is ill at Netherfield, that she should be outspoken in defense of her family when Lady Catherine assumes arrogant superiority: "In marrying your nephew, I should not consider myself as quitting that sphere. He is a gentleman; I am a gentleman's daughter; so far we are equal" (356).

Yet, when all is said in favor of Elizabeth's individualism, we recognize that the unfolding novel qualifies her position. Elizabeth is "disgusted" at Lydia's behavior following her wedding to Wickham: "Lydia's voice was heard in the vestibule; the door was thrown open, and she ran into the room"; a little later, Lydia "observed, with a laugh, that it was a great while since she had been there" (315). If the scene serves to underscore the consistency of Lydia's vulgar character, it also marks another stage in Elizabeth's and the reader's, awareness of the possible excesses of humor and playfulness. Wickham's "good humoured ease" as he inquires after his acquaintance in the neighborhood takes on a different "appearance" now than when it accompanied his slander-filled conversation with Elizabeth in Mrs. Phillips's drawing room.

Elizabeth had earlier come to an awareness of the possible abuses of laughter and wit in her conversation with Jane regarding the respective merits of Wickham and Darcy (225-226); and she has later to suffer through her father's ill-judged satire directed against Mr. Collins's letter warning of the imprudence of a match between Elizabeth and Darcy: "Elizabeth tried to join in her father's pleasantry, but could only force one most reluctant smile. Never had his wit been directed in a manner so little agreeable to her" (363). It is, therefore, no surprise, following Darcy's proposal, that she should check her own tendency to score a witty point: "She remembered that he had yet to learn to be laught at, and it was rather too early to begin" (371).

Of course the novel does not require Elizabeth to suppress her "lively, sportive manner of talking," only to regulate it through tact, consideration for others, and a measure of social decorum. Georgiana Darcy is still to be astonished, almost alarmed, at the "open pleasantry" directed at her elder brother by Elizabeth, and the reader is left hoping that the shades of Pemberley will be polluted by Elizabeth's occasional use of homely speech, that in spite of what the grammarians might say, she will continue to keep her breath to cool her porridge. For, if one of the lessons of this beautifully balanced novel is that the extremes of wit, humor and spontaneity are "ecstasy," "rapture" and immorality, another is that the opposite qualities of seriousness, correctness and respect for tradition have their own extremes of pomposity and social or moral conformism. If Elizabeth learns not to laugh, or to run, quite so often, and to temper her tendency to outspoken comments, Darcy, for his part, learns to smile occasionally, to adopt a less rigid mien, and to add a measure of ease to his conversation.

In the above analysis I have moved from an initial consideration of Lydia Bennet in terms of her substandard speech to a view of her less as a "character"—though that she is the presentation of a headstrong, selfish, highly sexed fifteen-year-old only theoretical pedants would deny—than as a complex of motifs or thematic repetitions whose meanings derive from their existence in the system of language that is *Pride and Prejudice*. Nothing outside the work can satisfactorily account for the combination in Lydia of her laughter, loud voice and running, though it is possible to connect her immoderate mirth to the "mirth of the mob" that Lord Chesterfield found distasteful and warned his son against, and it would doubtless also be possible to find in contemporary conduct books sufficient grounds for deprecating her indecorous tendency to excessive noise and motion. Helpful as such external "sources" are, however, Lydia's speech and behavior are mainly significant in relation to the speech and behavior of Elizabeth, Mrs. Bennet, Mary Bennet, Wickham, and all the other "characters" or clusters of signs in the novel.

The interpretive principle that might be invoked here against K. C. Phillipps states that Jane Austen's fictional language requires synchronic rather than diachronic analysis. Since the terms are voguish as well as useful, it may be as well to say that many of the best Austen critics have observed the principle without, to my knowledge, invoking or even thinking of Ferdinand de Saussure. Saussure's theories are nevertheless of much current interest, and their importance for Russian formalism, structuralism of various denominations, and the "science" of semiology, of which Roland Barthes is the chief proponent, can hardly be overestimated. In a consideration of Jane Austen's "meaning," moreover, it may be that they have an important place.[8]

Saussure's leap was from a substantive to a relational mode of thinking about language. Insisting that language be viewed as a total system existing for the native speaker at a moment in time, he gave the term *langue* to the total system of language postulated and the term *parole* to the individual speech utterance. By a perhaps too easy extension subsequent critics of literature have treated individual texts as *paroles* existing within *langues* considered as totalities of various kinds: the language system of the author's culture, literature viewed as a body of simultaneously existing terms, even the total written output of the author himself. What the extension of Saussure's theories into literary interpretation has permitted is a differential or diacritical view of a text's meaning. If a historical grammarian like K. C. Phillipps is interested in the semantic changes occurring to words through time, the interpreter influenced by Saussure is interested in literary texts as systems of signs, and he insists that "signs" are wholly arbitrary. For Saussure, "the linguistic sign unites not a thing and a name, but a concept [*signifié*] and a sound image [*signifiant*]" (*Course in General Linguistics*, p. 66). Words are not intrinsically meaningful. Sense is communicated and understood through an awareness of the relations and differences between the smallest sound units, though for the critic of the novel, if not of a short poem, an awareness of the relations and differences between words will probably suffice. Considered as an extended *parole*, the language of a given novel may be viewed as a "code," or series of "codes," giving patterned significance to words that, in themselves, are without given meaning.

My previous analysis of Lydia's "character" in terms of motifs inextricably woven into the patterned tapestry of *Pride and Prejudice* was intended to give some support to such a "relational" view of meaning. Yet I recognize that such a view collides with one of the most widely sanctioned opinions among Austen critics, namely that her words, especially her conceptual nouns, carry "substantive" weight. C. S. Lewis found many to agree with him when he wrote in "A Note on Jane Austen" (1954): "The great abstract nouns of the classical English moralists are unblushingly and uncompromisingly used; *good sense*, *courage*, *contentment*, *fortitude*, 'some duty neglected, some failing indulged,' *impropriety*, *indelicacy*, *generous candour*, *blamable distrust*, *just humiliation*, *vanity*, *folly*, *ignorance*, *reason*. These are the concepts by which Jane Austen grasps the world. In her we still breathe the air of the *Rambler* and *Idler*. All is hard, clear, definable; by some modern standards, even naïvely so." In short, and in apparent contradiction of Saussure, Jane Austen's *signifiants* identify *signifiés* that, far from being arbitrary, are "hard, clear, definable." Though the contradiction is more apparent than real, it has the merit of identifying a current task facing critics of Jane Austen, which, it might be suggested, is to find ways of reconciling the necessity of "diacritical" analysis of her novels with a sense of the embodied presence in her texts of, if not absolute, then common or received moral standards. In another sense, the task could be defined as the search for a criticism which, while accepting and indeed celebrating a plurality of significances, can yet argue convincingly for a measure of "closure" in the novels, a closure that is both intended by the author and exempt from Barthes's charge of "ideology."

III

As a start, one may say that though C. S. Lewis's brief for Jane Austen's use of hard and definable concepts is open to qualifications, such qualifications need not destroy the force of the claim.

Qualifications *are* necessary. Just as "wit" and "good humour" depend for their meaning on the contexts in which they appear or the characters with whom they are yoked, so the great abstract nouns are known by the company they keep. Stuart Tave has recently insisted that "there are few 'good' words or 'bad' words in Jane Austen's lexicon, as there are relatively few things good or bad in themselves. Persons, places, times, circumstances, manners, motives will determine. . . . One cannot simply say, for example, that 'propriety' is one of Jane Austen's values, but 'sensibility' is not, because as they stand those statements have no useful truth or falsity" (*Some Words*, pp. 30-31). But Tave's apparent support of a "relational" view of Jane Austen's words is itself qualified by other arguments that make more "substantive" claims and, indeed, give support to Lewis's argument. In Jane Austen, Tave writes earlier, "language is *a given reality* that presents choices and so tests the powers and the life of its users by their ability to make the right choices. . . . As time and space are not subject to individual desires but are *determinate realities, measurable by public standards*, words are the defined means by which men and women speak and hear not a private or imagined meaning but *the reality common to society*" (p. 21, my italics). Moreover, though Tave is properly reticent about the interpretive value of his eighteenth-century glosses, these tend to give strong support of Lewis's view that in Jane Austen "we still breathe the air of the *Rambler* and *Idler*." Mrs. Chapone is cited on "disposition," Thomas Reid on "sense" and "nonsense," Gisborne on "fortitude" (a very persuasive gloss this; see Tave, pp. 283-284); but it is Johnson on the "imagination" which preys incessantly on life, or on the need for "truth" in daily life, who is most frequently and approvingly cited.

The mediation (rather than contradiction) in Tave's study between "relational" and "substantive" modes of thinking about Jane Austen's language may be felt to come close to the kind of accomodative criticism I have suggested is necessary. In many ways Tave's study is excellent. No one, to cite but one example, has talked so convincingly of Jane Austen's attitude to marriage, a subject often inadequately summarized in the formula (Lord David Cecil's, I think) that while in her novels it is wrong to marry for money, it is stupid to marry without. By focusing on a single word, *affection*, and then by working out from the debate between Elizabeth and Charlotte in *Pride and Prejudice* to other novels, the fragments and the letters, Tave patiently builds up (pp. 131-141) a whole picture of Jane Austen's views on "conjugal felicity." All the relevant evidence, one feels, has been brought together. As a result, I am persuaded of the normative force in Elizabeth's criticism of Charlotte following the latter's acceptance of Collins (*PP*, 135-136). Charlotte is not to be excused for preferring Mr. Collins and an establishment to a penurious single life; the moral compromise she makes—not to mention the prudential shifts she is driven to at Hunsford parsonage—is too great. Elizabeth may give her credit for her powers of co-existing with her husband, but in the larger view her marriage, devoid of affection, is to be deplored.

But Tave is not always so successful, and it is worthwhile asking whether his method, which is to be "digressive on the word," is at fault. Words for Tave are colored strands to be followed through the texture of Jane Austen's works. The assumption is that "her world is so fully and integrally shaped, in a vision that sees the whole and the smallest part, that one can touch it anywhere and begin to trace *the* pattern" (p. xi). The italics I have added to this sentence make clear that, unlike Barthes, Tave evidently believes in the objective validity of the meanings his method "produces." Understanding Jane Austen so thoroughly, steeped for decades in her novels, he seems to speak for or through the author herself. As the dust-jacket blurb puts it: "his critical ego is everywhere subordinated to the task of revealing what *Austen* meant, what *Austen* said."

But did Austen mean what Austen said? The question is begged whether we can express critically what an author "says," and, beyond this, the equation of meaning and statement would trouble theorists as different as Cleanth Brooks and Roland Barthes. One of the deficiencies of Tave's largely admirable study is that his critical metacommentary frequently borders on the "heresy" of paraphrase (cf. pp. 82-96) or of direct quotations without quotation marks (passim). Though I would argue against the thrust of Barthes, Kermode, and Wolfgang Iser, that aesthetic value is not necessarily to be equated with textual indeterminacy, it seems true that even a "classic" author like Jane Austen will leave, in Iser's formula, indeterminacies to be repaired in her works.[9] Whether the critical repair of indeterminacy generates meaning (as Iser argues) or points to aesthetic failure on the author's part only specific instances can determine. The problem novel *Sense and Sensibility* may be briefly considered in this respect.

The problem of *Sense and Sensibility* is, of course, Marianne Dashwood. Critics have differed widely over the nature and success of her characterization. For some she is a heroic nonconformist resisting the hypocritical conventions of society, an insurgent but finally betrayed part of Jane Austen herself. For others she reveals, in her pursuit of the mediated code of sensibility, the immoral and ultimately irreligious implications of a morality finding its sanctions in the feeling heart. Still others, notably Walton Litz, have argued for a middle view and have seen the deficiencies of the novel as aesthetic rather than personal, as stemming from the failure to integrate inherited novelistic antitheses rather than as evidence of the betrayal of the author's finer instincts. Tave's argument (pp. 78-111) is surprisingly orthodox. Employing here a method of character analysis reminiscent of Bradley's Shakespearean criticism, he conducts what has to be termed a vendetta against Marianne. Of course there is ample evidence to show that Marianne is selfish, inconsiderate, and imperceptive of real feelings in others (in her sister, in Colonel Brandon, in Mrs. Jennings). But are we on this account to argue, as Tave does, that she displays "misdirected emotion" in her response to Willoughby during the agonizing scene of their meeting in London (*SS*, 176)? Are we really meant to stress a similar misdirection of emotion in Marianne's praise of Elinor's screens following Mrs. Ferrars's pointed neglect of them in the drawing room of her house in Harley Street (235-236)? And are we to temper our sympathy for her when she barely suppresses screaming on receipt of Willoughby's letter (182) because of the "agonies displayed, with less justice, on earlier and smaller occasions" (Tave, p. 80)? To argue thus is surely to substitute cold analysis for affective response, and Marianne—there can be no doubt—does inspire affective response in readers, even those who see her as a fallible figure responding to experience in accordance with the spurious principles of an artificial code. The immediate and continuing agony she experiences as a result of Willoughby's betrayal is surely as genuine as her criticism of the fatuous Mrs. Ferrars is merited—however outspoken in the mouth of a seventeen-year-old and however embarrassing to Elinor. The deficiency of Tave's method, at least in the instance of *Sense and Sensibility*, lies in his insistence on cutting a single pattern (*the* pattern) from the whole cloth. *Sense and Sensibility*, we are told, "is the story of Elinor Dashwood." But why be so categorical?

What if there are a number of patterns in the text? What—for the moment allowing Barthes provisional assent—if *Sense and Sensibility* is of interest to us precisely because it resists objective interpretation and invites the production of multiple readings? In *S/Z*, that extraordinary two-hundred-page commentary on *Sarrasine*, a twenty-page story by Balzac, Barthes distinguishes five codes interwoven in the text. Two of these, the hermeneutic and the proaïretic (or actional), are, as Kermode argues, linear codes that respectively unravel the plot and unfold "generic" sequences of action (examples of the latter in *Sense and Sensibility* might include "the encounter" and "the sick-bed"). Two others, the endoxal and the semic, encode cultural and thematic information. Most important to Barthes is the symbolic code or "field": "ce champ le lieu propre de la multivalence et de la réversibilité" (*S/Z*, p. 26); and the principal task of the critic is to show that one may enter the symbolic field by several different but equally valid entrances, which complicate the work's resonance, rendering it "problematic," and therefore authentic.

It would be fair to say, I think, that though Tave shows interest in patterns that resemble in certain ways Barthes's semic and cultural codes, he has little interest in interpreting a symbolic code in *Sense and Sensibility*. Where Barthes values multivalence and reversibility in a work of fiction, Tave seeks determinacy. Where Barthes uncovers layers only to find more layers, Tave seeks and finds a kernel of meaning. What Austen says Austen means, if the critic is skilful enough in tracing the whole pattern. But *Sense and Sensibility* has a way of resisting single patterns and determinate readings, and it does seem to possess a symbolic code. One has no way of knowing whether Tave read Tony Tanner's introduction to his Penguin edition of the novel (1969)—since he has regrettably dispensed with footnotes, bibliography and index in his book—but the presumption must be that he did not; if he had, he would surely have been led by Tanner's brilliant interpretation to take a less moralistic attitude toward Marianne's "violence" and to have been more sympathetic to her muffled scream at the center of the novel.

From its first sentence ("*Sense and Sensibility* is, of course, about sense and sensibility, but it is also about secrecy and sickness") Tanner's interpretation bears the mark of his reading in Freud and Foucault, and one's initial reaction is to consider his introduction an exercise in the discovery of the "relevance" (or *Sinn*) of Jane Austen's novel at the expense of its "meaning" (or *Bedeutung*).[10] Though such a reaction is never wholly eradicated, the brilliance of Tanner's textual analysis deftly supports his general argument that the novel's subject is the "drama precipitated by the tensions between the potential instability of the individual and the required stabilities of society" (p. 9). One merit of this analysis is that it can account for the most anomalous of details; another is that, in a manner suggestive of Barthes, it reveals the interweaving of several codes in the novel. When Edward Ferrars, about to propose to Elinor at last, seizes a pair of nearby scissors and, in his embarrassment, cuts the sheath to pieces as he speaks (*SS*, 360), Tanner reads this curious incident as the appropriate action of a character who has led a life of "*fettered* inclination." Again, Tanner notes how appropriate it is that Elinor, who tries to "screen [Marianne] from the observation of others," should herself be a painter of screens. Marianne, of course, neither screens her outrage nor fetters her inclinations, but for Tanner no simple verdict is invited. Though Elinor's self-control is admirable and morally superior to Marianne's "outbursts," we cannot fail to sympathize with the latter's anger against Mrs. Ferrars, "which means that Jane Austen has brought us to the point of feeling some positive approbation and appreciation for both the maintainer of screens and the discarder of screens" (Tanner, pp. 16-17).

Tanner's interpretation does not revive the view that Marianne is the true heroine of the novel, betrayed not by Willoughby but by her author. He recognizes, with Ian Watt and others, that Jane Austen accepts her society as an unalterable given. But, in asking us to remember "the scream behind the screen, the scissors straining against the sheath," he points to symbolic dimensions of the novel, ignored or minimized by Tave, that are surely important to its meaning. It is here that the parallel with Barthes may be cautiously drawn. Like Barthes, Tanner often proceeds by uncovering one layer to discover another, so that by an easy transition one may move from his insights to Barthes's methods. Thus in the scissors scene Barthes would surely have no trouble discovering the presence of at least three codes. There is an actional code (the proposal is a unit in the Richardsonian novel); there is a hermeneutic code (the scene occurs precisely at the moment of *dévoilement;* Elinor only now discovers that Edward is released from the "sheath" of his engagement to Lucy and "free" to marry her); and there is a symbolic code (the "Freudian" significance of the scissors cutting the sheath at the moment of proposal needs no explication).[11]

It would, however, be wrong to exaggerate the parallels between the methods of Tanner and Barthes. While the two critics are alike in their sensitivity to symbolic resonances, Tanner's essay gives no hint of an acceptance of extreme structuralist assumptions. He believes, one assumes, in existence of *signifiés* as well as *signifiants* in *Sense and Sensibility*. If the novel is not a nut whose kernel can be easily extracted, then neither is it an onion the peeling of which reveals "nothing except the infinity of its own envelopes." He may see in his text a tissue of self-referring signs, but he does not deny that the novel is the predicated expression of a psychological and moral subject, Jane Austen. He may come close (sometimes perilously) to Barthes's critic as producer, rather than consumer, of meanings; but he does not deny the importance of authorial intention, though he may view "intention" as a less explicit set of signals than Tave. Recognizing and indeed valuing indeterminacy in the object of his analysis, Tanner nevertheless seeks and finds determinate meanings.

IV

If I have suggested as a normative sequence of rising steps the movement from "substantive" to "relational" to "symbolic" readings, I must now begin to qualify this suggestion, and, indeed, come some way back down the ladder. And if I have preferred Tanner's reading of *Sense and Sensibility* to Tave's, this preference must not be taken to indicate a general endorsement of the former's methods. Of Tanner's three Penguin introductions, those to *Mansfield Park* and *Sense and Sensibility* seem to me superior to the one to *Pride and Prejudice*. Tave, for his part, is excellent on *Pride and Prejudice* and *Emma.* Tanner, it would seem, is better with the "problem" novels, whose tensions and indeterminacies leave larger "gaps" for his creative intervention. Tave's criticism, on the other hand, works better with novels which, though they still invite very different readings, seem to most readers more finished, more "classical," under more authorial control. These remarks may serve as prelude to my first qualification, which is of any extreme emphasis on the enigmatic nature of Jane Austen's fictional language.

The qualification may best be made through a consideration of Frank Kermode's two articles, already cited, which are splendid examples of the kind of engagement with Barthes and French structuralism that we may expect and welcome in future Austen criticism. Kermode's interest in Barthes stems no doubt from the challenge the latter has posed to his definition of *classic. Classic* for Kermode is a value term defining works which persist through time, *not* because they embody eternal values (this "imperial" definition is a sure way of disqualifying a work for classic status, since the "eternal" values of one age are likely to be rejected by the next), but precisely because they are philosophically and ideologically "reticent" and imprecise. Barthes, on the other, uses *classic* in a pejorative sense (as an antonym of *modern*) to define works which are precise, which limit meaning, which effect "closure." "What Barthes calls 'modern,' " says Kermode, "is very close to what I am calling 'classic,' and what he calls 'classic' is very close to what I call 'dead' " ("A Modern Way with the Classic," p. 431).

We should hesitate before too quickly concurring with Kermode's witty summation. Stripped of its pejorative content, Barthes's definition, after all, is closer to what is usually thought of as a classic than Kermode's. Kermode begins by opposing Barthes but ends up, in carrying Barthes's insistence on an unlimited plurality of significances back to certain great works of the past, agreeing with him. If Barthes would concede that great works of any period have the same unrestricted openness to the production of interpretations (and he comes close to this in *S/Z*), if he would admit that the distinction between *lisible* and *scriptible* is evaluative rather than historical, then Kermode would have no quarrel with him, and would indeed rejoice in their common mission of secularizing the old view of the classic, seeing it now "in all its native plurality, liberated, not extinguished, by death—the death of writer and reader—unaffected by time yet offering itself to be read under our particular temporal disposition" (p. 434). Clearly, there is more agreement here than opposition.

A real opposition to Barthes might grant the rough accuracy of his definition of "classic" and then try to disarm its negative intention. The texts Kermode chooses in his attempt to rehabilitate the classic against Barthes's charges of aesthetic and ideological closure are *Wuthering Heights* (in "A Modern Way") and Anthony Burgess's *MF* (in "The Use of Codes"). He admits that the latter choice might be objected to on the grounds that it is a modern work, but claims he could have met that objection by speaking instead about *The Scarlet Letter*. I wish he *had* treated *The Scarlet Letter*, but I would have been even more pleased if he had interpreted *Tom Jones*, or *Pride and Prejudice*, or *Emma*. For though both *Wuthering Heights* and *The Scarlet Letter* are "classics" in one sense, in another—Northrop Frye's—they are "romances," special forms of prose fiction characterized by their ineffability. And, if Frye's argument that the romance is a more revolutionary form than the novel is accepted, then Kermode's choice of texts is even less suitable as a test of Barthes's theory, for the latter, presumably, would have little trouble in seeing Brontë and Hawthorne as precursors of modern multivalence.[12]

To put the matter briefly: one might say that Kermode, in attempting to oppose the classic-modern antithesis, fails to take account of another antithesis of equal force, that between classic and romantic. *Pride and Prejudice* and *Emma* are classic, not romantic, novels. They possess the qualities found in ancient Greek and Roman art by the German critics of the late eighteenth century, *Heiterkeit* and *Allgemeinheit*. There is "closure" in these works, but such closure is to be viewed as the classical virtue evidenced when the form contains and defines, rather than blurs and suggests, meaning, when a sense of serenity and general fitness emerges from the particularized frictions of the plot or design. It is a closure that reflects a faith that there is order, in spite of abundant appearances to the contrary, embedded in the scheme of things. In Jane Austen, this faith, whose ultimate "origin" is religious, is not complacent; indeed, it is often threatened, as parts of *Sense and Sensibility* and *Persuasion* may reveal. Many readers prefer these works in which emotional forces seem about to break down formal restrictions, just as many prefer Chartres to the Parthenon, or *Wuthering Heights* to *Tom Jones*. But there are many, too, who would agree that in at least two of her novels Jane Austen gave classical expression to a vision of the world whose shape and values, however pungently expressive of her own nature, find their source in the traditions of Christian rationalism.[13]

Such a view, of course, runs counter to the structuralists' dislike of closure, dismissal of the author as rhetorical subject, and denial of "origins." It is, therefore precisely the kind of common (and to me, valid) view that may need defence in future Austen criticism. I would hope that the defense would not take the form of Kermode's capitulation to pluralism or seek, through an extreme reverence for the "constitutively ambiguous" nature of Jane Austen's language, to turn her into a classic of the modern sort, freeing her texts from her responsibility and control, laying their (not her) stylistic devices bare, and discovering in her novels systems of *signifiants* sans *signifiés*. For such a "defence," surely, would seriously misrepresent the "classic" character of a novel like *Pride and Prejudice*. To expand on the point, we can briefly look at two of the best existing interpretations of the novel. Taken together, these interpretations, it might be proposed, provide the kind of critical accommodation between "substantive" and "relational" emphases that I called for earlier.

First, there is Samuel L. Kliger's "Jane Austen's *Pride and Prejudice* in the Eighteenth-Century Mode" (1947), of which R. W. Chapman wrote in his *Critical Bibliography* that it was "open to the familiar objection that its subject would not have understood it." It would have been more appropriate to write that Kliger understood Jane Austen better than she understood herself; for, in his demonstration of the importance of the art-nature antithesis to the novel's characterization and dialogue, Kliger placed *Pride and Prejudice* in a detailed context of eighteenth-century aesthetic and ethical debate, of which, certainly, Jane Austen would have had little explicit knowledge, but which, even so, provided and continues to provide one of the most illuminating entrées to the work. Kliger's "hermeneutic" recovery is not, of course, a total reading, but taken together with an article that respects the novel as a system of self-referring signs and internally generated meanings—I refer to Reuben Brower's "Light and Bright and Sparkling: Irony and Fiction in *Pride and Prejudice*" (1951)—it convinces me that a valid and determinate interpretation of the novel is possible. Brower's article is an example of the kind of analysis which, knowingly or unknowingly, respects Saussure's "relational" view of language. No one, moreover, could be more aware of the novel's ironies and ambiguities. Indeed, in a phrase that reminds us of Barthes, Brower speaks of the "simultaneity of tonal layers" in the early conversations between Elizabeth and Darcy. But Brower insists that Jane Austen's "ironies are linked by vibrant reference to basic certainties." Thus, while he demonstrates Jane Austen's expressed awareness of the difficulty of knowing another ("knowledge of a man like Darcy is . . . a construction, not a simple absolute") he denies that the novel's vision is "one of Proustian relativity." There are certainties signified, concepts embodied, and, to recall the title of another article by Brower, these are directed by the author's controlling hand.

Pride and Prejudice is so perfectly structured in accordance with authorial intentions, its resolution so beautifully "closes" the plot, that it is difficult to see how the linguistic structuralist could avoid damning it as a classic in Barthes's sense. True, it would be possible to approach the novel, in structuralist fashion, not as a consciously shaped form finding its material in earlier novels and traditions of aesthetic and ethical debate, but as "a kind of extension and application of certain properties of Language." Indeed, if one were to pervert the intention of Tzvetan Todoroff's paper on "Language and Literature," it would be possible to provide just such a reading of the novel.[14]

Todoroff's argument, simply stated, is that literature imitates not life, nor even previous literature, but language itself. Thus a Boccaccio novella can be seen to have the form of the rhetorical figure of syllepsis, and the structure of characterization in *War and Peace* can be understood in terms of the stylistic features of parallelism and antithesis. An application of this approach to Jane Austen's early novels, whose very titles suggest the author's interest in questions of synonymy and antonymy, could have interesting, if somewhat predictable, results. Synonymy may be defined as two linguistic forms sharing the same content: thus we are told that Mrs. John Dashwood finds Lady Middleton "one of the most charming women in the world," and Lady Middleton, of course, returns the compliment. These characters are synonyms of "sense" defined as "a kind of cold hearted selfishness" (*SS*, 229). Absolute synonymy, however, is not possible in language; so Mrs. Dashwood is "a strong caricature of [her husband];—*more* narrow-minded and selfish" (5, my italics). Then, to cater for inexact synonymy, the principle of "gradation" is needed: thus in *Pride and Prejudice* Lady Catherine, Mr. Collins, Mary Bennet, Darcy (to name no more) are all gradations of "pride," ranging from an arrogant extreme of "improper" pride to a potential for proper pride, a potential, however, that will only be defined when the term is "qualified" by its "proper" antonym.

Antonymy complicates the semantic concept of gradation, requiring the extra notion of an "echelon" structure. At the end of *Pride and Prejudice,* as many teachers who use blackboards know, Darcy and Elizabeth stand together at the head of what may be termed diverging lines of semantic deterioration.

A detailed extension of this kind of analysis would not be futile. Norman Page (pp. 78-79) has drawn our attention to the late eighteenth-century interest in the "drawing of fine distinctions between words of approximately similar meaning." He cites no fewer than six works, of which Mrs. Piozzi's *British Synonymy* (1794) is the most well known. Mary Bennet, of course, is an adept in the mode. And it could be argued that Jane Austen herself, in a much more subtle way than Mary, of course, structured her characterization and positive moral vision in *Pride and Prejudice* through the drawing of fine distinctions that are ultimately verbal in kind. Gilbert Ryle, in support of his view of Jane Austen as an "Aristotelian" moralist, makes something like this argument in his "Jane Austen and the Moralists" (1968). But such an emphasis on the basically linguistic configuration of Jane Austen's early fiction is, as I have intimated, a perversion of Todoroff's argument, for it assumes Jane Austen's conscious manipulation of semantic similarities and differences. Todoroff's argument, by contrast, is that language itself (the ultimate determinant of all semiotic systems) imprints its structures on literature. There seems to be no bridge to cross here.

Jane Austen, we might insist, using theoretical terminology she certainly would not have understood, is fully aware of the "relational" nature of linguistic meaning. It is perhaps the central insight of the early works. The danger to her (rather than fact) of a purely arbitrary relation between signifiers and signifieds, sound and concept, is what motivates much of her irony. "How were people, at that rate, to be understood?" (*NA*, 211). The answer may be found in a description of a major intention of her writing, which is, it may be said, to reachieve in her fictional world the "substantive" meanings equally absent from her real life and the inferior fiction that she read. She it is, rather than the reader, who seeks to repair indeterminacy.

V

A word must be said in conclusion of the mature novels, for it could be argued that, though it may be possible to view *Pride and Prejudice* positively as a "classic," *Mansfield Park*, *Emma* and *Persuasion* resist the definition and lay themselves open to *écriture* of the most authentically unrestricted kind. Certainly these works go beyond the antithetical checks and balances of the earlier novels. There is a new interest in symbolism, or in what, following Howard Babb, we may term the emblematic method. When we think of these works, it is often to recall the "staged" scenes, taking place outside or during a "scheme" of one kind or another: the great Sotherton sequence in *Mansfield Park*, the picnic at Donwell Abbey and the trip to Box Hill in *Emma*, the walk to Winthrop or the events at Lyme in *Persuasion*. Then again, these works differ markedly in the handling of point of view and the sophistication of the free indirect style. Their greater complexity and resonance is not only to be admitted, but celebrated.

This is not to say, however, that we should abandon "hermeneutic" goals in favor of the search for multiple codes interwoven in these texts. Jane Austen's codes, I have suggested, work centripetally not centrifugally. Symbolism, in her instance, however resonant and resistant to critical paraphrase, is not a field of "reversibility." The claim can only be stated here, not supported, though by asking the reader to recall, or refer to, Joseph M. Duffy (1956), or Charles Murrah (1958), or Lloyd Brown (1973) on the symbolic significance of the Sotherton scenes, or to Trilling (1957) on the view of the Abbey Mill Farm from Donwell Abbey, or to Richard Poirier (1966) on the Box Hill episode, I can have others support the argument for me better than I could do myself. These critics show how Jane Austen employs the emblematic method in complex but functional ways to support her moral and social vision. And it is certainly no slur of their efforts to suggest, for example, that more can be done in the way of an appreciative understanding of her choreography of figures and groups, or of her tendency to set her figures in situations of an almost allegorical character, in which double entendre is transformed from vulgar social witticism to become the mark of a morally vitiated mind.

Not all Jane Austen's symbolism, of course, is of this emblematic kind, and not all her critics are appreciative. Some have looked for symbolism of a more psychologically revealing sort. There is no doubt that it is there. In an interesting article, "Jane Austen and the Stuarts" (1968), Brigid Brophy makes much of a sense of social degradation she believes afflicted Jane Austen from her early days, a sense exacerbated by the relative impecuniousness she, her sister, and mother felt on the removal from Steventon and on the later death of the Rev. George Austen. This sense can be discovered in the letters and the fiction, most obviously in the description of Fanny's claustrophobic reaction to the smallness of the rooms and the thinness of the walls at Portsmouth. Miss Brophy's observation is keen and her use of biography valid. My objection is not that biographical or psychological facts are used to account for features in the literary text, but rather that Brigid Brophy has not taken the method far enough. She suggests that Jane Austen's sense of frustrated entitlement is abandoned when Emma is educated out of the "family romance" and fantasy of high pedigree she projects onto Harriet Smith. But can we not argue that Jane Austen's continuing concern with degradation, with the loss of social "title," informs *Persuasion*, too, a novel in which the theme of "accommodations" may be seen as a conscious elaboration and authentic working out of the unconscious threat correctly identified by Miss Brophy? Mrs. Smith's "noisy parlour, and dark bedroom behind" in Bath,

Captain Harville's tiny rooms in Lyme, Mrs. Croft's uncomfortable accommodations in the man-of-war—these, along with the "renting" of Kellynch Hall and the absence of a final "estate" for the heroine, suggest that Jane Austen in her last novel accepted the reduction of earlier dream horizons and faced the exigencies of her life with the same spirit as Captain Harville, the same intention "to turn the actual space to the best account" (*P*, 98). One may argue, in this way, that even Jane Austen's unconscious (or partly conscious) symbolic structures in the later novels are capable of "limited" interpretation.

To do so, of course, is to invite the charge of *asymbolie* and to stand convicted of the associated crime of pursuing *la critique universitaire* with all of the concealed ideological assumptions that implies (unless Jane Austen is determined to be a "classic" in Barthes's sense, in which case I am right, but only at the expense of having Jane Austen's novels expelled from the canon of authenticity). The charge of ideology should be briefly considered in conclusion. It is an important one for critics to face, for it is not only a hypothetical structuralist objection to Jane Austen's fiction, but an existing fact of Austen criticism. Three critics, Arnold Kettle (1951, 1967), Graham Hough (1970), and Raymond Williams (1971), have argued that her social and moral vision is limited by, and works on behalf of, the class to which she belonged. Their sociological and antimoralistic emphasis is to be distinguished, however, from the structuralist objection I have hypothesized, and there seems to be a real possibility of an accommodation between their approach and academic approaches stressing scholarly backgrounds or the close analysis of stylistic features.

Kettle, Hough, and Williams *value* Jane Austen, though not for reasons often adduced. To say, as I have said, that she gives her personal stamp and a classic form to a cultural vision finding its roots in eighteenth-century reason and Christian principles would not to them be acceptable or, at least, enough. Kettle and

Williams would argue that this is to "mystify" her, to set up a smoke screen that conceals the real class basis of her social and moral vision. For them, her value lies in her ability to reflect and (though not consciously) interpret the concrete social reality of her time. Jane Austen has an important place in William's cultural history of England (most recently propounded in *The Country and the City* [1973]), for beneath the delicate surface of her pictures of domestic life in country villages Williams sees important reflections of that period of speculative interaction between landed and trading wealth in which the split between "culture" and "society" first seriously widened.

Hough's approach is not so much sociological as antimoralistic. Rather in the manner of Cardinal Newman who deplored the lack of a "high Catholic ethos" in Jane Austen, Hough once wrote of Jane Austen's morality that it was an "English middle-class version of Christian morals—Christian morals with all the heroism, all the asceticism, all the *contemptus mundi* left out." He has since valuably extended and qualified these views in the most challenging recent article to appear on Jane Austen: "Narrative and Dialogue in Jane Austen" (1970). A brief examination of this paper will provide an appropriate ending to this essay.

Hough's article is a fitting ending because, in his detailed stylistic analysis of Jane Austen's fiction, he discovers an intentional "coherence" in her work that is at odds—albeit unintentionally—with structuralist principles at every point. Thus: (1) There is no "reversibility" in her works: "In a Jane Austen novel the action, the characters, the values and the language all work in complete unison" (p. 220). (2) There is no constitutive ambiguity: "Her value judgments are clear and explicit; . . . they are not contradicted by the narrative; they are not ambiguous" (p. 220). (3) There is, however, closure, and of a most decided kind: "Her coherence springs from the will and the intelligence rather than from the deep unconscious roots of personality. . . . Coherence is attained by a deliberate limitation of possibilities" (p. 227).

(4) There is ideology: "I see the novels as strongly ideological constructions; . . . they are powerful reinforcements of a particular class structure and of a moral structure adapted to support it. The reinforcement is powerful because the moral structure is a strong and coherent one. . . . It has been fortified by elements from older and more world-embracing systems than its own—for it comprehends a secularized Christian ethics, a tinge of Johnsonian stoicism, all lightened by a gaiety that goes back to the heroines of Shakespearian comedy" (p. 227).

If we exempt the reference to Shakespeare, it would almost seem that Hough is acting as a structuralist inquisitor counting off the heresies before assigning Jane Austen's "classic" works to the flames. But, of course, Hough is not condemning her cultural vision but criticising it in the radical sense of the word. He sees her as contributing to that peculiar English reification of the nineteenth and early twentieth century which accepted the "values of the upper bourgeoisie as non-historical absolutes" (p. 228), and he wants Jane Austen's critics to be aware of this too.

With this kind of criticism there can be both disagreement and dialogue. Much more detailed work, it seems to me, needs to be done in the area Hough has himself investigated, that is, in the analysis of different kinds of discourse in her fiction, particularly her use of the free indirect style. Critics like Karl Kroeber and Norman Page have already begun to examine in detail this curiously neglected aspect of her art. (It is not before time: Willi Bühler's substantial study of *erlebte Rede* in Jane Austen came out in 1937). Kroeber in particular has interesting things to say about the role of the narrator in relation to the reader in her fiction. Unlike Charlotte Brontë's narrator, who, especially in her notorious addresses to the reader, feels compelled to assert a community she knows to be lacking, Jane Austen's narrator assumes an easy community with her readers. Such a community, sensed by present day readers, many of whom are neither English nor bourgeois, is not to be explained by claiming that these readers are accomplices in false consciousness. To pursue this argument, however, would not be to reject but to qualify Hough's proposals and to participate in the dialectic of critical inquiry. It is not yet clear to me that the implicit antitheses posed by French structuralism to the existing body of Austen criticism will result in satisfying new syntheses. *Hoc opus, hic labor est.*

NOTES

1. Douglas Bush estimates, in his *Jane Austen* (New York: Macmillan, 1975), that in the years 1923-1973 sixty-seven books on Jane Austen appeared, thirty-one in the last decade. Barry Roth and Joel Weinsheimer list 794 items in their *Annotated Bibliography of Jane Austen Studies: 1952-1972* (Charlottesville: University Press of Virginia, 1973).

2. Barthes puts forward the principles of his "nouvelle critique" in, among other works, *Critique et Verité* (Paris: Editions du Seuil, 1966) and *S/Z* (Paris: Editions du Seuil, 1970). A good brief account of his views on style may be found in "Style and its Image," in *Literary Style: A Symposium*, ed. Seymour Chatman (London and New York: Oxford University Press, 1971), from which I have taken the passage quoted in the second epigraph to this essay. *Critique et Verité* is Barthes's polemical reply to Raymond Picard's polemical attack in *Nouvelle Critique ou Nouvelle Imposture* (Paris: Les Editions Jean-Jacques Pauvert, 1965). Hugh Davidson, "Sign, Sense, and Roland Barthes," in *Approaches to Poetics*, ed. Seymour Chatman (New York: Columbia University Press, 1973), pp. 29-50, provides a useful, though pro-Barthes resumé of the *querelle* and a lucid account of Barthes's theoretical principles.

3. "The Use of the Codes," in *Approaches to Poetics*, p. 56. See also the same author's "A Modern Way with the Classic," *New Literary History*, 5 (1974), 415-434.

4. "Three Dimensions of Hermeneutics," *New Literary History*, 3 (1972), 246. The same issue of *New Literary History* contains Frederic Jameson's translation of Dilthey's "The Rise of Hermeneutics," from which I have taken the sentence quoted in the first epigraph to this essay.

5. Interested readers are referred to the index of Roth and Weinsheimer's *Annotated Bibliography* for the books and essays by these critics and for all works on Jane Austen alluded to in this essay but not footnoted.

6. K. C. Phillipps, *Jane Austen's English* (London: Andre Deutsch 1970); Karl Kroeber, *Styles in Fictional Structure: The Art of Jane Austen, Charlotte Brontë, George Eliot* (Princeton: Princeton University Press, 1971); Norman Page, *The Language of Jane Austen* (Oxford: Basil Blackwell, 1972); Lloyd W. Brown, *Bits of Ivory: Narrative Techniques in Jane Austen's Fiction* (Baton Rouge: Louisiana State University Press, 1973); Stuart M. Tave, *Some Words of Jane Austen* (Chicago and London: University of Chicago Press, 1973). I should also mention here David Lodge's *The Language of Fiction* (New York: Columbia University Press, 1966), valuable not only for its sensitive reading of *Mansfield Park* but for its long theoretical introduction, one of the few attempts in English or American criticism to consider explicitly the critical problems involved in the interpretation of novels.

7. For example, in his discussion of financial metaphors in Jane Austen's novels (pp. 65-66), Phillipps notes that Mark Schorer and Howard Babb have differed on the matter, Babb objecting that Schorer sees financial metaphors where they do not necessarily exist. Phillipps affirms their existence in Jane Austen but avoids pursuing the implications of their existence, preferring to change the subject by stating that metaphorical language is not commonly used in the novels except for ironical purposes. At issue here is the important question of whether the penetration of Jane Austen's English by financial terms vitiates her moral vision, or, at least, uncovers its fundamental class character.

8. Saussure defined synchronic linguistics as the study of "relations between co-existing terms of a language state," as opposed to diachronic linguistics, which is the study of "relations between successive terms that are substituted for each other in time" (*Course in General Linguistics*, ed. Charles Bally and Albert Sechehaye; trans. Wade Baskin [New York: McGraw, 1966], p. 140). For lucid expositions of Saussure's theories as they influence Russian formalism and linguistic structuralism, see Frederic Jameson, *The Prison House of Language* (Princeton: Princeton University Press, 1972). For a lucid brief account of Saussure and excellent introduction to structuralism, see

Edward W. Said, "Abecedarium Culturae: Structuralism, Absence, Writing," *Modern French Criticism: from Proust and Valéry to Structuralism*, ed. John K. Simon (Chicago: Chicago University Press, 1972).

9. See "The Reading Process: A Phenomenological Approach," *New Literary History*, 3 (1972), 279-299.

10. For a discussion of the distinction (originally Frege's) between *Sinn* and *Bedeutung*, and of related distinctions between "relevance" and "meaning" and "criticism" and "interpretation," see E. D. Hirsch, Jr., *Validity in Interpretation* (New Haven and London: Yale University Press, 1967), esp. appendix 1.

11. Cf. Barthes's discovery of five codes in a *lexie* from *Sarrasine*, in "Style and Its Image," p. 5.

12. Since finishing this essay, I find that Kermode *has* written briefly on *Tom Jones* and *The Scarlet Letter* in "Novels: Recognition and Deception," *Critical Inquiry*, 1 (1974), 103-121—another interesting, if often cryptic, attempt to domesticate Barthes and Derrida. Predictably *Tom Jones* is seen as a "production" to be consumed (and Fielding as an author who attempts "to prescribe the imaginative action of the reader"), while *The Scarlet Letter* is seen as a novel that not only permits but enjoins plural interpretation. The distinction, again, is between a work that is *lisible* and one that is *scriptible*, and, in terms of criticism, between *écrivance* and *écriture*. But Kermode's argument with respect to *Tom Jones* seems invidious, or at least incomplete. Granted that Fielding is an authoritative writer effecting formal and ethical closure in *Tom Jones*, the critical task would seem to be to defend such a narrative role against Barthes. Instead, Kermode spends much of his essay proving brilliantly that Ford's *The Good Soldier* is constitutively ambiguous. Few would doubt it, but then few would place it in the same class as *Tom Jones*.

13. A recent expression of this view will be found in Bush's *Jane Austen*.

14. Todoroff's paper is collected in *The Languages of Criticism and the Sciences of Man: The Structuralist Controversy*, ed. Richard Macksey and Eugenio Donato (Baltimore and London: Johns Hopkins Press, 1970), pp. 125-133.

KARL KROEBER

SUBVERTING A HYPOCRITE LECTEUR

> Only the non-real has the power to convert the real into sense, into meaning.
>
> Käte Hamburger

Not the least of the multiple ironies created by Jane Austen's art is the circumstance that her first novel to be sold was published posthumously. Then the most April-fooling of her fictions was linked to the autumnal *Persuasion.* But joint publication of her first and last, most lighthearted and sombre works was appropriate, generally because (as Lukács has observed) literary art reverses the causal sequences of life, and specifically because *Northanger Abbey*'s parody outlines modes by which Jane Austen's maturest fiction disengages her reader's imagination from conventionalized expectations. Nowhere is her exploitation of the facts and dangers of preconceiving better illustrated than by *Northanger Abbey*'s concluding absurdities.

> The anxiety, which in this state of their attachment must be the portion of Henry and Catherine, and of all who loved either, as to its final event, can hardly extend, I fear, to the bosom of my readers, who will see in the tell-tale compression of the pages before them, that we are all hastening together to perfect felicity. The means by which their early marriage was effected can be the only doubt. . . .

> The General, soon after Eleanor's marriage, permitted his son to return. Henry and Catherine were married, the bells rang and everybody smiled; and, as this took place within a twelve-month from the first day of their meeting, it will not appear, after all the dreadful delays occasioned by the General's cruelty, that they were essentially hurt by it. To begin perfect happiness at the respective ages of twenty-six and eighteen, is to do pretty well; and professing myself moreover convinced, that the General's unjust interference, so far from being really injurious to their felicity, was perhaps rather conducive to it . . . I leave it to be settled by whomsoever it may concern, whether the tendency of this work be altogether to recommend parental tyranny, or reward filial disobedience. (250, 252)

Among these jokes is the trickiest for novel-writers: to most of us, the "real" is what we expect. Exaggerating the conventionality of her conclusion, Jane Austen catches us out laughing at Catherine, who makes mistakes because of her assumptions as to how events will occur. Whatever their charm (and practicality among Italian mountains), Radcliffean presuppositions are inappropriate in central England, lacking wild scenery of towering peaks and abysmal chasms and their psychological equivalents—unmitigated purity and unmitigated villainy. If, like naive Catherine, we preconceive too gothically, we will miss actual good and bad abounding in "the midland counties" of life. The conclusion of *Northanger Abbey* should remind us that from the first Catherine's difficulties arise not from her fashion of seeing but from her fashion of foreseeing. Prefigurings warp her perceptions. What are disappointed are her overexcited expectations, and she is saved by lack of fantasizing imagination. Her innate tendency is to see things as they are. She is always inept at delusive preconceivings, a difficult disciple for Isabella. So the shape of the book's central joke is delineated in the opening chapter, describing Catherine's incapacity as a gothic heroine. She will never fully succeed in distorting actuality to fit literary patterns she's persuaded ought to be imposed on reality. She is a Victor Frankenstein manqué.

Her failure as a modern Prometheus means more than plain fun for the reader. If we are hastening together to perfect felicity, are we not in danger of ending where Catherine began? Are we not, finally, forcing reality into patterns we have learned to expect at the expense of what we should simply see? Fortunately, Jane Austen's irony is present to encourage consciousness of the dangers in conventional vision and thereby to save us from thinking *exactly* like Isabella Thorpe. Awareness thus aroused, however, reminds us how close all of us are to Isabella. The recognition enables us to laugh at Catherine and her silliness without contempt.

Such laughter is rare. Jane Austen has created a heroine persuasively "open, candid, artless, guileless, with affections strong but simple, forming no pretensions, and knowing no disguise" (206). Catherine keeps trying, but she remains a credulous listener rather than a storyteller, "unable to speak well enough to be unintelligible." Henry Tilney catechizes her on the appropriate response to Isabella's jilting of her brother:

> "You feel, I suppose, that, in losing Isabella, you lose half yourself; you feel a void in your heart which nothing else can occupy. . . . You feel that you have no longer any friend to whom you can speak with unreserve; on whose regard you can place dependence; or whose counsel, in any difficulty, you could rely on. You feel all this?"
>
> "No," said Catherine, after a few moments' reflection, "I do not—ought I?" (207)

Catherine feels, Henry assures her, "what is most to the credit of human nature," and he goes on to describe the central purpose in all Jane Austen's fiction: "such feelings ought to be investigated, that they may know themselves" (207). Such dialogue between guileless listener and artful teller reinforces the primary structure of *Northanger Abbey*, aimed at ridiculing not so much gothic fiction as its audience. *Northanger Abbey*'s lighthearted but decisive condemnations are more than literary criticism, because the novel subverts preconceptions of a gothic-trained readership. In this regard *Northanger Abbey* is prophetic, for our relation to the action in Jane Austen's novels is never as simple as her lucidly tactful style, her superlative writing manners, tempts us to believe. When we think of the difficulties each of her heroines encounters with parents, we realize that the first novel's last words forecast a recurrent ambiguity, the question of whether the plots, all of them, "recommend parental tyranny, or reward filial disobedience." In each novel a core situation is some kind of parental power confronting some form of filial revolt, because each focuses on the overthrow of some conventional distortion of reality—and in that distortion/overthrow the reader's awareness is involved.

If "not much happens" in Jane Austen novels, much happens outside them, partly through their unusual attention to expectations. The thoughts and imaginings of the chief characters are directed predominantly toward the future. Catherine's adolescent anticipations of Bath and the Tilney estate foreshadow the schemes, plans, hopes, estimates of possibilities of the other heroines, who insistently look ahead. The protagonists' psychology is reinforced by narrative order: fewer words are devoted to actions than to preparations for actions. The theatricals in *Mansfield Park* may serve as grand illustration: *Lovers' Vows* is never performed. More significant is the retrospective *Persuasion*, filled with detailed anticipations—yet Wentworth's so fearfully expected return occupies only a sentence. Anticipation plays so large a role in Jane Austen's plots and in the minds of her protagonists because it is her principal theme and a key mode for liberating her readers' imaginations from the confinement of their preconceptions about reality.

Catherine Morland is silly because of the way she foresees: she imagines events will occur in a manner incongruous with patterns of "midland county" life. Because Emma Woodhouse is not silly, is closer to the center of British civilization, she is more dangerous; anticipating the sentiments of others, she would impose misalliances on all Highbury. If Emma joins Catherine and Marianne Dashwood, three romantics who must temper their delusive predictive tendencies, on the opposite side Elinor Dashwood, Elizabeth Bennet, Fanny Price, and Anne Elliot find their all-too-sensible expectations upset. Their judicious assessments that they have no chance to marry, respectively, Edward Ferrars, Fitzwilliam Darcy, Edmund Bertram, and Captain Wentworth, turn out as wide of the mark as the calculations of the too imaginative heroines. The crystal balls of sense and sensibility are equally clouded. For Jane Austen as emphatically as for tragedians of fifth-century Athens, life is uncertain.

Her classicism needs stress, if only to loosen the misleading label often gummed to her fiction: novels of manners. Of course manners count. Manners control how events happen; manners make life predictable; in a well-mannered society nothing untoward takes place, and the excitement which attracts us to sensational fiction will be unknown. But let us remember, if Catherine Morland learns that Mrs. Radcliffe is not a perfect guide to midland realities, she also gains a well-mannered husband who admires Mrs. Radcliffe's fiction. To Jane Austen the civil virtues are circumscribed by the danger that civility will eliminate the uncertainties that are life. This danger the happy ending of *Northanger Abbey* (like that of subsquent novels) proves to have been overcome. One couple at least breaks the confining assurances of conventionalized manners to reach a more-than-conventional actuality. Who, after all, could have forecast that Catherine would become Mrs. Henry Tilney? Astonishing—like all good marriages. Specially astonishing, Catherine's lover is a Henry gifted with a sensibility comparable to that of his creator. As I'll observe shortly, she is not uncritical of her protagonist, but the very complexity of his virtues suggests that if Jane Austen is to be called a novelist of manners, the term indicates her awareness that they are inadequate, however essential, to full human possibilities. "Politeness,"

John Fowles remarks, "always conceals a refusal to face other kinds of reality."[1] Tilney's "charm" is that his politeness implies, when it does not enunciate, irony toward conventions of civility.

Northanger Abbey sets the pattern for Jane Austen's form. Each of her novels concludes with a happy ending, so that we may recognize the limits of that convention. Thus, ambiguously concluded is not only the story of a heroine's education but also a lesson for the reader, a shaping of his awareness of the assets and deficits in the preconceptions he brought to the novel. Elizabeth catches Darcy's attention by behaving contrarily to what is expectable from a penniless young lady with a chance at a husband worth ten thousand a year. He secures her affection by proving how little conventional behaviour appropriate to his station can determine the actions of a man genuinely in love. Crucial to their mutual learning, as to the equally unpredictable reversion into love of Wentworth and Anne, are facts of sensory experience, physical perceptions. Understanding the reality-shaping power of psychological preconceptions, Jane Austen used few words for sensory descriptions, but she knew the danger of habits of thought detached from sense experience, of manners separated from perceptible facts. Not surprisingly, she was peculiarly sensitive to the tendency of language to distort perceptual actuality. Henry Tilney has been praised for sharing Jane Austen's taste for verbal precision. But in her story his linguistic accuracy is played off against Catherine's commonsense and perceptual literalness. If Catherine sometimes misuses words, Henry sometimes misuses his senses. She defends herself against his criticism of her words:

> "You think me foolish to call instruction a torment, but if you had been as much used as myself to hear poor little children first learning their letters and then learning to spell, if you had ever seen how stupid they can be for a whole morning together, and how tired my poor mother is at the end of it, as I am in the habit of seeing almost every day of my life at home, you would allow that to *torment*

> and to *instruct* might sometimes be used as synonimous words." (109-110)

Catherine's language is founded upon what she has seen and heard, and the danger in Tilney's verbal agility is its tendency to ignore or distort facts. Shortly after her defense of her semantics Catherine, under Henry's tutelage, "voluntarily rejected the whole city of Bath, as unworthy to make part of a landscape." So much for actual perceptions. This is Tilney's absurdity. Jane Austen's more impressive heroes are not talkers, valuing most of all perceptual accuracy and truth to sensory facts. Mr. Knightley's comment upon Emma's portrait of Harriet Smith is exemplary: "You have made her too tall, Emma" (48). Funnier and more passionate but equally factual is Darcy's rejoinder to Caroline Bingley's sneer:

> "I remember, when we first knew her in Hertfordshire, how amazed we all were to find that she was reputed a beauty; and I particularly recollect your saying one night, . . . 'She a beauty! I should as soon call her mother a wit.' But afterwards she seemed to improve on you, and I believe you thought her rather pretty at one time."
>
> "Yes," replied Darcy, who could contain himself no longer, "but *that* was only when I first knew her, for it is many months since I have considered her as one of the handsomest women of my acquaintance." (*PP*, 271)

The perfect Austenian detail in Darcy's heart-warming rejoinder is "one of."

Her concern with exactness of language dependent upon a conservative estimate as to what words can do—and her belief that they ought never to be used to muddle our perceptions—helps to explain why Jane Austen began her career with parody. Parody focuses on style of expression, particularly distorting style, and (in all these ways differing from satire) looks forward, because it does not rely on accepted standards. Thus in ridiculing gothic romance, *Northanger Abbey* defines not what novels had depicted but what they ought to depict: something more than the novelty of romance. Presenting adventures in a foreign, exotic, "new" world, romance assures hero and audience of surprises, the foreknowledge that we and he are unprepared for what will happen. In romance, both protagonist and reader know they cannot know what to expect—hence anticipation plays a small or superficial role. *Frankenstein* may be thought a pure romance, since a monster by definition is not according to rule, is essentially outside convention. The classical novel, contrarily, works with and through conventions of both language and behaviour, subverting our preconceptions to free us from their tyranny, a tyranny inadvertently confirmed by the surprises of romance.[2] If (as is often said) the romancer is concerned with what might be, and the novelist with what is, the value of the distinction lies in the fact that "is" consists largely in what one is prepared to admit exists.

The romancer asks only a willing suspension of disbelief: then the Ancient Mariner, a green blob from outer space, or Frankenstein's monster may appear. The classical novelist confronts—and thereby affronts—what psychologists call the "set" of our expectations, how we perceive because of our predeterminations of what can and cannot happen, what we will see because of what we are disposed to see and to overlook. Romance does not challenge our "set," because it focuses upon the new, the original, the surprising, by definition that for which we are unprepared, about which we have no preconceivings. The realism distinguishing novel from romance is not a report of what we already know but a revelation that what we already know is inadequate to what we may experience—in fact, not just in fancy. The classical novelist is not interested in green blobs from outer space because he wants us to recognize not what might exist but what does exist, if we will only allow ourselves to perceive it. Novelistic realism expands our awareness of reality.[3] The cliché that truth is stranger than fiction is, curiously, the paradox upon which the classical novel is founded—which is why novelists from

Cervantes on have so often attacked other fictions with their fiction, as romancers do not.

Today the absurd sanities of *Northanger Abbey* are of more than antiquarian concern because they enable us to estimate to what degree modern taste may be hostile to the spirit of the classical novel. Such an estimate, giving insight into how willing or unwilling we are to having some of our preconceptions disturbed, is useful for judgment on the aesthetic success of earlier novels. I have suggested that Jane Austen does not present many sensory details because her fiction works to break down the fictions by which her reader limits his sense of what is real. She aims at the psychological patterns which determine how we perceive. It may be that the most popular forms of contemporary literature, fantasy, surrealism, science fiction, and their polar counterparts, such as the "nonfiction" novel, emphasize sensory details because they reinforce rather than undermine accepted ideas about "essential reality." The idea is worth entertaining that few modern novelists transform our assumptions about the nature of things, and that even the violence-into-perversity characteristic of our fiction, pretending to shock, in fact confirms the dominant belief that only sensory experience is "truly real."

The conviction that actuality is found only in the realm of sensory experience is, of course, evidenced by the violent sensuality of our fiction; but higher in the throat, so to speak, it is also evidenced (and I think more importantly) in efforts to reduce language to degree zero, that is, to the mode of the nonlinguistic. A surprising number of our fiction writers and critics compete in demonstrating that reality is nonverbal: our age is characterized by *S/Z* criticism of *M/F* fiction.[4] A prevailing critical dogma is that artistic language must *be* sensual experience. It has for many been a sign of the novel's aesthetic impurity that it tends to mean rather than be. A classical novelist would be shocked by this attitude toward language. Don Quixote's head was turned not by sensory facts but by the language of romance, the same disease infecting Catherine Morland. Cervantes and Jane Austen are in agreement that one can take fiction too literally, because imagination possesses the power to modify how we perceive. These classical novelists recommend careful distinctions between the linguistic and the nonlinguistic, and they locate the potency of language in its inappropriateness as a substitute for sensory experience. Language ought not to strive to be like physical perceptions because language can speak directly to imagination. Language, therefore, can arouse imaginative modifying and extending of sensory capacities (or restricting and obscuring of them), but it cannot properly act as a surrogate for sensation. In brief, to the classical novelist linguistic structures must primarily mean, not be.

This obsolescent psycholinguistics brings into focus the radical transformation worked by twentieth-century novelists through their exploitation of late nineteenth-century naturalistic principles. Empirical, positivistic naturalism assumed primacy of sensory reality, and that assumption contributed to later identification of the significant as the archetypal. Since one sensation is not intrinsically superior to another of the same force, repetition of sensation makes it special: the more often we have a "good" feeling the better, in a vulgar philosophy. One subtler form of this quantified value system is appeal to mythic pattern: a particular experience is seen as reformulating a fundamental, that is, many times reenacted, schema of behavior. Codified repetition is ritual, and for much twentieth-century literature significance resides in ritual. As T. S. Eliot observed in an early review of *Ulysses*, Joyce's writing was bound to be paradigmatic for modern literature because he had devised a method for finding mythic significance in "the immense panorama of futility and anarchy which is contemporary history." That panorama was of course described by (was indeed to a degree the creation of) post-Victorian naturalists, such as Zola, Moore, Maupassant, a generation older than Joyce. He surpassed these predecessors by archetypalizing the trivial, mundane actions of the least heroic segments of civilization, particularly the lower middle classes. His representation of natural contingencies as possessing the significance of ritual behavior made it difficult for his contemporaries to understand his work, their confusion reflected in later critics' uncertainty as to how to classify his books. But his "mythicism" in fact fulfills by restructuring the naturalistic ideals he inherited. Unlike Eliot, Joyce does not retreat finally to a suprasensory metaphysic, and he does not appeal to any meaning beyond the archetypalism found *in* the most ordinary kind of sensory experience.[5] This is why his writing is characterized by peculiar attention to verbal sound, to language *as* aural experience.

In 1975 we need something like the contrast of the Irish innovator who could call himself Jeems Joker to savor in the classical art of *Northanger Abbey* the conventionality of its language. Challenging rather than reinforcing its readers' conceptions of actuality, concentrating on the mind behind the speaking voice,[6] the classical novel cannot attempt a Joycean synthesis of sonic harmonies and mythic patternings. Its primary order must derive from the aesthetically conventional; it must be submissive to arbitrary rules of syntax and vocabulary. But by overtly, even ostentatiously, submitting (the basic technique of parody), it may lure our attention to the distinction between linguistic and sensory realms of experience. As I have suggested, the blatant conventionality of *Northanger Abbey*'s last pages does not so much close off as disclose a happy future of ambiguous significance—less because we are doubtful as to the work's attitude toward parental tyranny or filial disobedience than because we are presented with a challenge to any easy estimate of the function and value of fiction. This open ending carries over to the offensive Jane Austen's earlier defense of the novel in her novel. Her fight, like the "argument" of *Don Quixote*, is for commitment to the potential freedom of experience, belief that significant acts are not only re-enactments, that art can improve our psychic powers. Her spirit is antithetical to the Joycean philosophy (so representative of our age) of *plus ça change, plus la même chose*. If we do not confuse literature with living, we can learn from literature to think more clearly, feel more intensely, and behave more generously.

The classical novel aims to influence nonliterary experience by enriching our capacities for imagining reality by spoiling our preset system of responses. The classical novel is vitally, not merely literarily, ironic. By displaying the inadequacies of existent conventions, it implicitly affirms that we can be masters of such conventions, not, like the Thorpes (and in a different fashion H. C. Earwicker), their slaves. The conclusion to *Northanger Abbey* is so splendidly hilarious because it crystallizes Jane Austen's novel-long exposure of the quintessential hypocrisy of novel-readers, a pretense of not taking novels seriously to conceal a tendency to take them all too literally.

> "I am no novel reader–I seldom look into novels–Do not imagine that *I* often read novels–It is really very well for a novel."–Such is the common cant.–"And what are you reading, Miss–?" "Oh! it is only a novel!" replies the young lady; while she lays down her book with affected indifference, or momentary shame. . . . Only some work in which the greatest powers of the mind are displayed, in which the most thorough knowledge of human nature, the happiest delineation of its varieties, . . . are conveyed to the world in the best chosen language. (37-38)

NOTES

1. *The Magus* (New York: Dell, 1965), p. 106.

2. My use of the term *classical novel* derives from a broad study of shifting relations between fictional and social realities, of which this essay forms a part. I apply the term to most novels written before the last quarter of the nineteenth century, principally as a convenience for contrasting the "modern" novel, here summarily

represented by Joyce. Both terms *classical* and *modern* of course subsume complexly diversified subdevelopments.

3. Thorough investigations into the use of "realism" as a critical idea have been conducted by René Wellek; see especially "The Concept of Realism in Literary Scholarship," *Concepts of Criticism* (New Haven: Yale University Press, 1963), pp. 222-255. Because novels are about realities not recognized, they are instrinsically "subversive," and this may be why there are so many fine novels by women. They have been in an excellent situation for perceiving realities which the masculine "set" of society does not want to admit.

4. George Steiner is unusually explicit but entirely representative in observing: "It is no paradox to assert that in cardinal respects reality now begins *outside* verbal language" (*Language and Silence* [New York: Atheneum, 1967], p. 17). He can point, for example, to the "radical distrust of language" in so exemplary a modern intellectual as Levi-Strauss (p. 249).

5. C. G. Jung's "*Ulysses:* A Monologue" interestingly defines the apparently contradictory mythic/naturalistic features of Joyce's art. Jung sees *Ulysses* as an essential *document humain* of the twentieth century "because it is *not* 'symbolic'" in the sense of expressing "something whose nature we cannot grasp." *The Spirit in Man, Art and Literature* (Princeton: Princeton University Press, 1971), pp. 123-124.

6. Alan Spiegel, in an essay tracing the evolution of descriptive techniques in "realistic" fiction from Flaubert to Joyce, points out that vision in *Ulysses* is "cold" and "camera-like" because Joyce specializes in descriptions in which "vision" is separated from the "process of inner life that lies behind it." But in actuality, Spiegel observes, "we do not only see with the eyes, but with the mind as well. We see . . . what we desire to see, what the mind allows us to see." "Flaubert to Joyce: Evolution of a Cinematographic Form," *Novel: A Forum on Fiction*, 6 (1973), 241. The classical novelist cannot undertake such cinematographic description because his language is ordered to influence the structuring mind behind the perceiving eye.

JOSEPH WIESENFARTH

AUSTEN AND APOLLO

The best recent critical writing on Jane Austen has come out of an interest in history. Avrom Fleishman's investigation of evangelicalism, the economic difficulties of the gentry, and the abolitionist movement in the second decade of the nineteenth century has shed light on Sir Thomas Bertram's once enigmatic voyage to Antigua in *Mansfield Park.*[1] Alistair Duckworth's identification of the estate as a metonym for society as whole, for a code of morality, a body of manners, and a system of language, has by an analysis of politics and landscape gardening given a dimension to Austen's canon that was lacking before *The Improvement of the Estate* was published.[2] Lloyd Brown has placed Jane Austen's rhetoric within traditions exploited by Locke, Hume, Burke, Shaftesbury, Swift, and Johnson, and illuminated her use of irony, image, and parody.[3] Jane Nardin has focused her attention on the meaning of propriety in *Those Elegant Decorums* and shown how Austen's novels can reasonably be read as the drama of giving moral definition to a traditional concept in new and changing contexts.[4] Stuart Tave has studied the repetition of some words of Jane Austen to provide a lexicon of their meaning in her time.[5] Critical essays have shown an awareness of history, though perhaps not as much as scholarly books, and I single out Duckworth's essay on *Mansfield Park* as the one that best furthered our understanding of a single novel by historical investigation,[6] and Brown's essay on the feminist tradition as the one that best furthered our understanding of the entire canon.[7] If the voice of B. C. Southam, raised in "General Tilney's Hot-Houses,"[8] is heeded, historical study of Jane Austen will continue to take root, burgeon, and delight.

I do not intend, however, that this essay should further the reading of Jane Austen's novels by a dive into history. I intend it as a dip into the murkier waters of myth in her fiction. To my knowledge Geoffrey Gorer was the first one to scull Jane Austen around the rivers of the underworld in "The Myth in Jane Austen," an aberrant but popular essay published in 1941.[9] The essay was popular because it fastened the dream patterns of young Jane's disturbed psyche upon her later novels. The essay was aberrant biographically because it did not add a fact to her life, and aberrant esthetically because it treated the novels as symptoms of a more serious disorder within the novelist herself. Gorer's reading of Jane Austen depended on the novelist's being psychologically disturbed, and her being psychologically disturbed depended on the novels reading the way Gorer said they did. In short, what Gorer needed evidence for, he made evidence for. Jane Austen's family life, the exegesis went, was unhappy and insecure; therefore she later created in each novel, save *Persuasion*, a heroine "who hates and despises her mother and marries a father-surrogate." Gorer extended this argument in 1957 in an essay significantly entitled "Poor Honey: Some Notes on Jane Austen and her Mother."[10] Suffice it to say, speaking for myself, that myth's first incursion into Jane Austen's world did nothing to further my understanding or appreciation of that world.

The next foray of the "anthropological-psychological" method into the "occult structuring" of Jane Austen's novels was Douglas Bush's madcap essay "Mrs. Bennet and the Dark Gods: The Key to Jane Austen."[11] Herein Bingley becomes Dionysius, god of the dance; Mr. Bennet becomes Pentheus; Mrs. Bennet, his Maenad mother; and Darcy, Tiresias. But when Bush realizes that Mrs.

Bennet was born by the sea ("she is a native of Meryton, the town of *mare*, the sea") and that Mr. Bennet stalks books in his library, he knows that she is Venus and he is Adonis and that, in such a context, Mr. Collins, with the entail favoring him, is the dangerous marauding beast: "We have here what is perhaps the most striking ambiguity in the book: Mr. Collins is both the Boar and the Bore (and his clerical status adds a further though unexploited element of traditional ritualism)." His role is later subtly assumed by Lady Catherine de Bourgh when Elizabeth and Darcy emerge as a younger Venus and Adonis.

Bush's happy parody was meant to head off myth-critics at the pass and decimate them with laughter. He was largely successful, because myth in Jane Austen never got the book that, at the end of his essay, Bush predicted it doubtless would get.

In Gorer and Bush we have the two extremes of total seriousness and total lack of seriousness in the application of a method to a subject; and the interesting thing is that each has just about the same amount of evidence and logic to prove his case. Neither is convincing, of course, because one distorts the novel for the sake of the method and the other distorts the method for the sake of the novel. A critic needs to respect both the integrity of the literary work he writes about and the usefulness of the method he employs to write about it. For Gorer the novel is a case-history; for Bush the method is madness. Gorer is so interested in the psychological content of myth that he forgets he is analyzing a novel, not a case-history. Bush so objects to the mythic approach as a method of literary analysis that he sidesteps what is in the novel to expose what is not, thereby destroying the method he distrusts. Gorer is Bush's "anthropological-psychological" critic who sees Austen's affinity with Kafka. Bush is Fleishman's "hostile critic [who] fails to see the unwelcome realities." Fleishman himself takes the approach of a literary critic willing to use any method that will expose dimension in a novel. He is the first critic of Jane Austen that I know of to use a mythic approach without converting a novel into a case-history and without distorting a method to destroy its usefulness (pp. 57-69).

I do not agree with all the points in Fleishman's analysis of *Mansfield Park*, but I see his approach as one that attempts to preserve the integrity of the novel, and I am satisfied, for the most part, with his conclusions. The way Fleishman works towards those conclusions is instructive because it exposes various facets of a mythic approach. Cinderella, "a universal figure in folklore," is related to "a more public and conscious realm" which concerns a struggle for property. Fanny Price is seen as Cinderella who "displaces her cousins in the heart . . . of Sir Thomas." This patriarch's choice of Fanny is related to Lear's choice of Cordelia and to Freud's essay on the Three Caskets and his *Beyond the Pleasure Principle*, so that Fanny represents life-denying values: "Her role is to deny the pleasures of life in favor of the pleasures of principle, which feel like death." The triumph of a virtuous Fanny and expulsion of a sinful Maria suggest that Mansfield Park is an earthly paradise: "It invites us to make friends with the necessity of guilt, misery, and death while holding out the possibilities of this-worldly salvation—a feeling of peace after the loss of vitality." Fanny, like children whom Carl Jung describes, "inherits the future and justifies the sufferings of the past."

The problem that I find with Fleishman's method is that before he convincingly examines the pattern of the Cinderella story he interprets its meaning through analogous myths and elucidations of those myths that sometimes relate only tangentially to the Cinderella pattern, which initially had not been carefully enough worked out. For instance, the pattern of the Cinderella story serves only Fanny Price's relationship with Henry Crawford, and not her relation to Sir Thomas and Edmund Bertram. *Mansfield Park* finally denies the actuality of the Cinderella myth and only affirms it as what could have been if Henry had been faithful to Fanny.

Could he have been satisfied with the conquest of one

> amiable woman's affections, could he have found sufficient exultation in overcoming the reluctance, in working himself into the esteem and tenderness of Fanny Price, there would have been every probability of success and felicity for him. His affection had already done something. Her influence over him had already given him some influence over her. Would he have deserved more, there can be no doubt that more would have been obtained; especially when that marriage had taken place, which would have given him the assistance of her conscience in subduing her first inclination, and brought them very often together. Would he have persevered, and uprightly, Fanny must have been his reward—a a reward very voluntarily bestowed—within a reasonable period from Edmund's marrying Mary. (*MP*, 467)

In other words, Fanny would have been Cinderella had Henry only persevered in being Prince Charming, but he did not.

One principle that emerges from taking issue here with Fleishman's procedure in analyzing an Austen novel is that when one recognizes a mythic pattern, that pattern should be worked out as clearly as possible before the archetypal implications of smaller configurations within that pattern are interpreted. For if the first step is not taken carefully, the second step may be taken mistakenly. Fleishman and I would undoubtedly reach the same conclusion concerning the child and the future, but I would get there by an analysis of mythic structure different from his.

The kind of discrimination that Francis Ferguson provides in his essay " 'Myth' and the Literary Scruple"[12] appeals to me as a way of proceeding when doing an analysis of myth. Following Malinowski, he distinguishes three kinds of myth: (1) *legends* or stories about the past believed to be true of the past; (2) *folk* or *fairy tales* or stories told only for fun, without reference to truth, simply for entertainment; (3) *religious myths* or stories which embody the basic elements in the creed, the morals, and social structure of a people. Jane Austen most often uses myths that entertain in the structure of her novels, the fairy tale "Cinderella" being one instance of that kind of myth. Her novels are, to be sure, the product of a mind and imagination that accepts the Christian myth presented in the Gospels as an immutable truth, and, logically, Jane Austen expresses in her novels a basically Christian ethic and worldview. But if one is interested in the patterns of structure in her novels, it seems more useful to begin talking about these patterns as they derive from myths which entertain and from there get to larger questions of value. Let us turn for a moment, then, to *Pride and Prejudice*.

Fitzwilliam Darcy, with £10,000 a year, meets Elizabeth Bennet, with £1,000 at 4% to her name, and refuses to dance with her. Darcy comes gradually to recognize more of what suits him in Elizabeth–her mother's least favored daughter–does dance with her at their next ball, shortly after seeks her out when she tries to avoid him, and offers her his hand in marriage. She refuses it. What Jane Austen sets before us in the first half of her novel are major elements of the Cinderella story, refusing, however, to allow the expected pattern of that story to be completed. Her refusal is instructive of her whole procedure in using well-known patterns of myth in her novels. She allows these patterns to fulfill the expectations they create only when they come to exist within a moral framework that satisfies her sense of what the true values in human life are. Darcy's proposal and Elizabeth's refusal allow the hero and heroine to understand each other completely, setting before them four problems that keep them apart: the problems of Bingley's separation from Jane, of Darcy's relation to Wickham, of the Bennet family's impropriety, and of Darcy's ungentlemanly manners. These problems have been built up dramatically section by section in the novel. Once stated, they must be removed dramatically before the novel can come to a conclusion. They are removed in the second half of the novel by Darcy's and Elizabeth's cultivating in themselves reason and empathy.[13] The function of this structure is to purge the hero and heroine of their illusions—to give them each self-knowledge so that they can see their good in each other. When they have achieved this open and affectionate condition, Jane Austen consciously begins her novel again in volume 3, chapter 12, by having Bingley return and by having Mrs. Bennet ask her husband to wait on him. *Pride and Prejudice* has what is analogous to a *da capo al fine* structure in music, with the novel beginning again in a new key, the key of reason and affection. Jane Austen seems in effect to be saying, "Now that Darcy and Elizabeth know what the truth is and now that they know they are each other's own best good, let's do everything again and see whether they can get the ending correctly this time." But just when everything suggests that Prince Charming is about to win Cinderella, Lady Catherine arrives to reintroduce all the problems. The luminous scene in which Elizabeth sends Lady Catherine packing is Jane Austen's insistence that intelligence and affection can overcome all obstacles to human happiness. Cinderella triumphs in spite of family and lack of money, and so does Elizabeth. Once the moral values are affirmed, the mythical pattern is completed.

The defeat of Lady Catherine is the defeat of conventional stupidity standing in the way of affection. As a de Bourgh, she never questions the rightness of the conventions which she insists Elizabeth must observe. Elizabeth, with ruthless logic, destroys any immediate relation between these conventions and human good. The Cinderella myth absorbs into its nineteenth-century embodiment in *Pride and Prejudice* a moment from the *Oresteia* to define its values more clearly. The moment has universal psychological validity, for the aspiring child must overcome the blocking parent to live a normal life.[14] Just as Orestes and Electra conspire together to kill Clytemnestra, Elizabeth, seconded by Darcy, overcomes Lady Catherine. We, the readers, like the Gardiners in the novel, celebrate this victory, just as Athena representing wisdom and Apollo representing order sanctioned the original deed of Orestes. This admirable victory of wisdom and order as represented by intelligence and affection gives the Cinderella myth a new concrete existence, showing that the exultation of dignity and reward embodied in its radical fairytale form can exist in 1813 if Prince Charming and Cinderella overcome the pride and prejudice within themselves and others that keep men from living happily ever after.

The same is not true of the Cinderella story in *Mansfield Park.* As the passage previously quoted from the novel insists, the achievement of satisfaction would have been possible if Henry Crawford had been faithful to Fanny, and he was not. The passage tells us all that could have been, but nothing that is. The Cinderella myth stands in the story as an indication of what has been thrown away. What is kept follows the pattern of another myth, that of Pygmalion and Galatea. The chaste and orderly Pygmalion, finding no woman suited to him, creates the statue of a perfect woman, falls in love with it, and by the indulgence of Venus has it come alive to be his bride. This more precisely represents the relation of Edmund to Fanny than the Cinderella story does. Having found Mary Crawford wanting, Edmund turns to Fanny, whom he has formed: "Loving, guiding, protecting her, as he had been doing ever since her being ten years old, her mind in so great a degree formed by his care, and her comfort depending on his kindness, an object to him of such close and peculiar interest, dearer by all his own importance with her than any one else at Mansfield, what was there now to add, but that he should learn to prefer soft light eyes to sparkling dark ones" (470).

Edmund marries the woman who most closely reflects his values in the novel, the woman whom he has unknowingly shaped from her youth to be his wife. Everything in the novel also makes it clear that Edmund, of all his father's children, is most like Sir Thomas in the values he professes, so that Fanny's relationship to Sir Thomas is also better defined by the Pygmalion story than by the Cinderella story: "Fanny was indeed the daughter he wanted. His charitable kindness had been rearing a prime comfort for himself. His liberality had a rich repayment, and the general goodness of his intentions by her, deserved it" (472). I would like to suggest that alongside the Cinderella myth in Jane Austen's novels, we place the Pygmalion myth as one of prime importance. I would like further to suggest that Cinderella is a radical story, tending to change social relationships once the marriage takes place and that Pygmalion is a conservative story, tending to preserve existing social relationships once the marriage takes place. Thus Lady Catherine objects vehemently to Darcy's marriage, visiting Pemberley after it only to determine whether the woods have been polluted by Elizabeth and her family; whereas Sir Thomas rejoices in what he once feared, that his niece would become his daughter. And Edmund and Fanny finally settle "within the view and patronage of Mansfield Park," there to preserve a way of life that they value in common with Sir Thomas.

The myths in Jane Austen coordinate with the radical and conservative tendencies of her novels, as I have defined them. The words *radical* and *conservative* are descriptive, not evaluative. There is no implication that *Pride and Prejudice* and *Persuasion* are better novels than *Mansfield Park* or *Emma* because the former are "Cinderella" and "radical" and the latter are "Pygmalion" and "conservative," or vice versa. Before going on to speak of *Emma* and *Persuasion* in this context, however, I want to say a word about *Northanger Abbey* and *Sense and Sensibility*. The pattern of the Pygmalion myth makes a rudimentary showing in each of these novels with Catherine Morland being formed in part by Henry Tilney's lecturing her, and with Marianne Dashwood being formed in part by Colonel Brandon, whose values are professed to Marianne by Elinor. In these novels the conserving voice is essentially male and recalls the would-be heroine from the chimeras of gothic fiction and romantic sensibility. In *Mansfield Park* the conserving voice is also male but needs to be educated by the heroine in the value of feeling. In *Pride and Prejudice* the radical voice is female, educating the hero in what it means for him to be a gentleman. So another consistent aspect of the "conservative" novel is the commanding moral position of the hero, and of the "radical" novel the commanding moral position of the heroine.[15] This is drawing things rather starkly and without shading, but it serves to set up rough categories as we proceed to the subtler effects of *Emma* and *Persuasion*.

Emma presents a vivid parody of the Pygmalion story in the heroine's taking the likeness of Harriet Smith. Emma is specifically interested in creating an elegant woman out of the "natural daughter of somebody," a project which Mr. Knightley sees as "errant nonsense." When one carefully examines the details of the portrait, one sees that Emma tries to give Harriet characteristics that Jane Fairfax, the novel's most elegant woman, already has: middle height, an improved figure, and eyebrows and eyelashes open to praise. Since Emma dislikes Jane, while admiring her elegance none the less, she tries to re-create that elegance in the awkward Harriet Smith. The portrait of Harriet is an exemplary instance of Emma's creating a fiction when she wants to ignore a fact. It epitomizes her conduct in matchmaking, which forever goes awry.

The making of a match for Harriet gives Emma a way of living her own emotional life vicariously, for Mr. Elton proposes to Emma, Frank Churchill flirts with her, and Mr. Knightley marries her; each of these men Emma had intended, at one time or another, to be Harriet's husband. When we return to Emma's portrait of Harriet, then, we also see in it the lineaments of the elegant woman Emma thinks herself to be. For the more closely Harriet's portrait resembles the elegance of Jane Fairfax, the more closely it resembles Emma's own elegance. The taking of the portrait of Harriet thus becomes the comedy of Emma's narcissism. In love with herself, Emma tries to create in Harriet an extension of herself which she expects society will respond to with the deference it shows her, and she also creates an emotional surrogate for herself whose romantic involvements she enjoys and suffers through more than Harriet herself does.

"Will you choose a wife for me? [Frank Churchill asks

> Emma at Box Hill]—I am sure I should like any body fixed on by you. . . . Find somebody for me. I am in no hurry. Adopt her, educate her."
>
> "And make her like myself."
>
> "By all means, if you can."
>
> "Very well. I undertake the commission. You shall have a charming wife." (373)

When Harriet finally marries Robert Martin—to whom Emma had initially objected and who had taken Harriet's exact measure on his wainscot before Emma had faultily taken her likeness—one sees that as a Pygmalion Emma is finally a thorough failure. But as a Galatea she is an unqualified success.

Emma plays Galatea to Mr. Knightley's Pygmalion:

> Till now that she was threatened with its loss, Emma had never known how much her happiness depended on being *first* with Mr. Knightley, first in interest and affection. . . . She had herself been first with him for many years past. She had not deserved it; she had often been negligent or perverse, slighting his advice, or even wilfully opposing him, insensible of half his merits, and quarrelling with him because he would not acknowledge her false and insolent estimate of her own—but still, from family attachment and habit, and thorough excellence of mind, he had loved her, and watched over her from a girl, with an endeavour to improve her, and an anxiety for her doing right, which no other creature had at all shared. In spite of all her faults, she knew she was dear to him; might she not say, very dear? (415)

Mr. Knightley rejects the notion that Emma herself is the answer to the conundrum which states that the two letters *M* and *A* equal perfection. He sees clearly that Emma is badly in want of perfection. He constantly corrects her misjudgments and reprimands her misdeeds until Emma realizes, as the passage just quoted shows, that Mr. Knightley has watched over her, improved her, and loved her. Mr. Knightley is a successful Pygmalion, whereas

Emma is not. Because her nature has possibilities that give direction to his art, Emma comes forth from his hands the elegant woman that Harriet Smith never had a chance of becoming. The counterpoint of the parody with the myth of Pygmalion, along with the extension of the parody in the myth of Narcissus, gives the novel not only psychological richness and subtlety, but also an underlying intelligibility and appeal.

Persuasion also uses a counterpoint of parody and myth in the Cinderella story, as well as extending the parody in the Narcissus myth. The least favored of three daughters, Anne Elliot has Lady Russell for a godmother who acts as stepmother. This stepmother encourages her to marry William Elliot, her father's rich and handsome heir, and thereby become Lady Elliot and duplicate in her own life the pattern of her mother's, who by marrying Sir Walter gained position and a title. But William Elliot, like Sir Walter, is a proud, callous man. If Anne were to follow in her mother's footsteps, she would accept a husband who is in his own way no better than her father. Now Sir Walter is carefully cast in the role of Narcissus and is madly in love with himself. Distinguished by his good looks and his title, Sir Walter makes Kellynch Hall into a house of mirrors in which to admire himself, and he makes the Baronetage his only reading because it reflects his family's prestige. For Anne to make a marriage that truly duplicates her mother's would be for Anne to enter into this pattern of narcissistic reflection, which, feeding upon its own images, cares nothing for the vitality of life outside itself. Therefore the pattern of the Cinderella story is not completed in the relationship between William Elliot and Anne; the story itself seems by nature too radical to be the foundation of a marriage that would preserve as far as possible a feudal way of life and a cyclic pattern of existence.

The vitality of England seen in *Persuasion* resides in its seafaring society, especially Admiral Croft and Captain Wentworth. Wentworth, who left Anne years before to go to sea a relatively poor man, returns a rich man. Harboring resentment against Anne because of her early refusal to marry him, he looks about to find a woman with constancy of mind and finds that Louisa Musgrove is a perfect woman until her constancy of mind leads her to fall on her head. Wentworth, in short order, realizes that Anne, his former lover, can be his only love: "Her character was now fixed in his mind as perfection itself, maintaining the loveliest medium of fortitude and gentleness" (241). Anne amazes her father, overcomes her godmother-stepmother, and astonishes her haughty sisters by accepting Wentworth's proposal. Poor in dowry as she is, she insists on being Cinderella, and Wentworth insists on being her Corsair-prince: "How should a Captain Wentworth and an Anne Elliot, with the advantage of maturity of mind, consciousness of right, and one independent fortune between them, fail of bearing down every opposition?" asks the happy narrator (248). The myth of Cinderella, as its pattern is completed by Jane Austen, remains the radical story of the fairytale version.

The way the fairytale is reworked further opens the novel to the consideration of a kind of mythic structure that seems to be new with Jane Austen in *Persuasion.* Like all of her novels, *Persuasion* is a comedy and therefore an embodiment of the mythos of spring.[16] What makes the comedy of *Persuasion* different from that of the other novels is that the blocking society is more closely associated with the forces of winter and death and the aspiring society more closely associated with the forces of warmth and life than heretofore. The aristocratic society in *Persuasion* is thoroughly moribund: static, artificial, self-serving, it casts a chill wherever it goes. Its image is the self-loving, death-desiring Narcissus. The seafaring society is dynamic, natural, and loving; it brings life from the very sea that threatens it with death. These dramatizations of life and death are more pronounced in *Persuasion* because it is more identified with a romantic world-picture than any previous Austen novel.[17] Anne reads Scott and Byron and discusses them with Benwick. She tends the flowers at Kellynch, prefers the country and its changing season to the city and its noise, and finds "bloom and freshness of youth" by the side of the same sea that gives Wentworth a career and a fortune. The "correspondent breeze," which M. H. Abrams has defined as a characteristic romantic metaphor,[18] fills his sails and puts color in her face. Futhermore, Wentworth at sea and Anne at home become introspective; and Anne, especially, is driven into that profound consciousness of self, "the strait through which everything must pass," in Geoffrey Hartman's words.[19] Anne emerges in the novel as an example, however rudimentary, of a consciousness and alienation that the romantic movement has made familiar to us all.

Having begun this essay with a recognition of the gains won by historical analysis for an understanding of Jane Austen's novels, and having further pursued an understanding of them through an analysis of patterns of myth, I would like now to suggest, with a few additional words on *Persuasion*, that neither method excludes the other and that both together can help us to a better sense of Jane Austen's meaning and value today.

As my comments on the romantic aspects of *Persuasion* suggest, Jane Austen shows an awareness of a new sensibility entering the stream of English history during the Napoleonic wars. The whole novel, in fact, shows a sense of history in its depiction of the rising importance of the navy and the declining importance of the aristocracy. The navy had saved England from invasion, preserved her West Indian holdings, and repeatedly frustrated Napoleon's forces. The aristocracy, however, did nothing comparable during this period. Kellynch-hall, representing the best of the English tradition, passes into the hands of Admiral Croft, with Napoleon's reluctant tribute to the British navy ringing in our ears: "Wherever there is water to float a ship we are sure to find you in the way."[20] Wentworth's accumulation of fortune at sea also represents Jane Austen's knowledge of the naval practice of awarding substantial shares of captured and sunken enemy vessels to victorious British officers. At the same time that navy men were growing rich, aristocrats were complaining to Pitt of high taxes and condemning his practice of raising new men to the peerage. In the vitality and success of Admiral Croft and Captain Wentworth and in the stasis and failure of Sir Walter and William Elliot, Jane Austen accurately reflects the history of her time.

Jane Austen's dramatization of a changing society in the second decade of the nineteenth century not only accords with historical fact but also presents the overarching myth of life itself in the conflict of Eros with Thanatos. *Persuasion* awards the victory to Love only to worry it a minute later by the shade of Death: Anne "gloried in being a sailor's wife, but she must pay the tax of quick alarm for belonging to that profession which is, if possible, more distinguished in its domestic virtues than its national importance" (252). The harsh political world of warring powers sits on the threshold of tenderness and affection. Her imagination tempered by history, Jane Austen knew that Napoleon would escape from Elba the very month that Anne and Wentworth were engaged. History touches *Persuasion* from beginning to end. To deny its power at the close of the novel would be to deny that the struggle of Anne and Wentworth in the changing world had value—to deny that "Anne deserves her Wentworth and Wentworth deserves his Anne."[21] To the very end, the new order meets the old, Cinderella affronts Narcissus, Eros challenges Thanatos in a world touched by history. To the very end history shapes the context in which Jane Austen works out the myths of *Persuasion*.[22]

The largest historical context in which Jane Austen's novels can be viewed, however, is that of Christian myth. The New Testament incorporates a religious myth of the kind that Fergusson described as representing the basic elements in the creed, morals, and social structure of a people. Jane Austen clearly believed in the Christian narrative and professed the values implicated in it. One need only read her evening prayers, each of which concludes with the "Our Father," to see how closely she attends to the

Trinity, the Incarnation, redemption, providence, and the fallen state of man. This last leads her to petitions such as these: "Teach us to understand the sinfulness of our own hearts, and bring to our knowledge every fault of temper and every evil habit in which we have indulged to the discomfort of our fellow-creatures, and the danger of our own souls."[23] We can hardly escape seeing that the characters in her novels are victims of the very faults from which she prays to be delivered. The novels are seldom explicitly religious, though some Christian instances do peep through. In drawing up her indictment against Darcy, for instance, Elizabeth never finds him "irreligious." Darcy even ends his famous letter to her by saying, "God bless you," and she later reminds him that "the adieu is charity itself." The novels are more often implicitly Christian. One has only to compare Mr. Knightley's relationship to Emma with the words of the prayer quoted above to see that he shows the sinner her own heart and teaches her the harm she does to herself and others.

The structure of comedy itself, moreover, as Northrop Frye has shown, has an archetypal pattern that is congenial to the Christian view of life:

> A serious interest in structure . . . ought naturally to lead us from *Pride and Prejudice* to a study of the comic form it exemplifies, the conventions which have presented much the same features from Plautus to our own day. The conventions in turn take us back into myth. When we compare the conventional plot of a play of Plautus with the Christian myth of a son appeasing the wrath of a father and redeeming his bride, we can see that the latter is quite accurately described, from a literary point of view, as a divine comedy.[24]

It should be noted that in the realm of archetypes the stories of Pygmalion and Cinderella are displacements of the myths of creation and redemption, respectively. So that if I am correct in postulating that Pygmalion and Cinderella are primary myths that appear as structural patterns in the novels, they are logically congenial to the Christian world-picture in which Austen conceives her characters and events.

Finally, it is well to remember, comedy predates divine comedy and has a pagan origin. The god that presides over comedy, if we can believe Nietzsche, is Apollo. He is the god of order, reason, and the dream. Apollo casts over the world the illusion that intelligent and affectionate people can control the destructive, tragic impulses of Dionysius and live relatively happily ever after. To be sure, this is a dream, says Nietzsche, but a dream which "make[s] life possible and worth living."[25] To each man it is left to determine whether he will accept the dream or not. But as long as Jane Austen's novels are read, Apollo will live and his dream will not die.

NOTES

1. *A Reading of Mansfield Park: An Essay in Critical Synthesis* (1st ed. 1967; Baltimore and London: Johns Hopkins Press, 1970), pp. 19-42.
2. Baltimore and London: Johns Hopkins Press, 1971.
3. *Bits of Ivory: Narrative Techniques in Jane Austen's Fiction* (Baton Rouge: Louisiana State University Press, 1973).
4. Albany: State University of New York Press, 1973.
5. *Some Words of Jane Austen* (Chicago: University of Chicago Press, 1973).
6. "*Mansfield Park* and Estate Improvements: Jane Austen's Grounds of Being," *Nineteenth-Century Fiction*, 26 (1971), 25-48.
7. "Jane Austen and the Feminist Tradition," *Nineteenth-Century Fiction*, 28 (1973), 321-338.
8. *Ariel: A Review of International English Literature*, 2 (1971), 52-62.
9. *American Imago*, 2 (1941), 197-204; rpt. *Five Approaches to Literary Criticism*, ed. Wilbur S. Scott (New York: Collier, 1962), pp. 91-98.
10. *London Magazine*, 4 (1957), 35-48.

11. *Sewanee Review,* 64 (1956), 591-596; rpt. Douglas Bush, *Engaged and Disengaged* (Cambridge, Mass.: Harvard University Press, 1966), pp. 20-26.

12. *Sewanee Review,* 64 (1956), 171-185; rpt. *Myth and Literature: Contemporary Theory and Practice,* ed. John B. Vickery (Lincoln: University of Nebraska Press, 1966), pp. 139-147.

13. An extended discussion of structure can be found in my *Errand of Form: An Assay of Jane Austen's Art* (New York: Fordham University Press, 1967), pp. 60-85.

14. For an analysis of the *Oresteia* myth in psychological terms, see Rollo May, *Man's Search for Himself* (1st ed. 1953; New York: New American Library, 1967), pp. 108-119.

15. For conclusions similar to these, arrived at from a different kind of analysis, see Brown's article.

16. See Northrop Frye, *Anatomy of Criticism: Four Essays* (1st ed. 1957; New York: Atheneum, 1967), pp. 163-186.

17. Northrop Frye, *A Study of English Romanticism* (New York: Random House, 1967), pp. 4-49, identifies the characteristics of a romantic world-picture.

18. "A Correspondent Breeze: A Romantic Metaphor," *English Romantic Poets,* ed. M. H. Abrams (New York: Oxford University Press, 1960), esp. pp. 51-52.

19. "Romanticism and 'Anti-Self-Consciousness,'" *Romanticism and Consciousness: Essays in Criticism,* ed. Harold Bloom (New York: Norton, 1970), p. 51.

20. Quoted in Michael Lewis, *The History of the British Navy* (Harmondsworth: Penguin Books, 1957), p. 133.

21. Paul Zietlow, "Luck and Fortuitous Circumstance in *Persuasion:* Two Interpretations," *ELH,* 32 (1965), 195.

22. For an extended analysis of this dialectic in the novel, see my "Persuasion: History and Myth," *The Wordsworth Circle,* 2 (1971), 160-168.

23. *Minor Works,* ed. R. W. Chapman (1st ed. 1954; London: Oxford University Press, 1958), p. 453.

24. *Fables of Identity: Studies in Poetic Mythology* (New York: Harcourt, Brace and World, 1963), p. 34.

25. Friedrich Nietzsche, *The Birth of Tragedy and The Genealogy of Morals,* trans. Francis Golffing (Garden City, N.Y.: Doubleday Anchor, 1956), p. 21.

JULIET McMASTER

LOVE AND PEDAGOGY

"Your lessons found the weakest part," Vanessa complained to her tutor Cadenus, "Aim'd at the head, and reach'd the heart." Swift and Vanessa weren't the first couple, nor yet the last, to discover that the master-pupil relationship can be a highly aphrodisiac one.[1] From Heloise and Abelard to Eliza Doolittle and Henry Higgins, history and literature produce recurrent examples of relations that evolve from the academic to the erotic. And Austen's novels afford in themselves a range of possibilities in the operations of teaching and learning as an emotional bond. As Lionel Trilling points out, Jane Austen "was committed to the ideal of 'intelligent love,' according to which the deepest and truest relationship that can exist between human beings is pedagogic. This relationship consists in the giving and receiving of knowledge about right conduct, in the formation of one person's character by another, the acceptance of another's guidance in one's own growth."[2]

Jane Austen, in exploring this subject so thoroughly, perhaps sets a standard for the nineteenth-century novel, which continued, partly because of its strongly didactic intention, to present love stories in which the heroine falls in love with a man who is her tutor, or her mentor, or her superior in age, experience, or authority. No doubt there is an Oedipal element in the relationship: the daughter is sexually attracted to the embodiment of her father's loving rule.[3] But society generally condones and even encourages this attitude, where it usually looks with disapproval or disgust on the young man who marries the older woman, however wise she may be.

Charlotte Brontë, although she despised Jane Austen for what she considered her failure in the depiction of passion, nonetheless fastened on the same central relationship for her most passionate attachments. Mr. Rochester is "the master," and Jane, equal soul though she is, looks up to him from the stance of servant, daughter, pupil:[4] "I love Thornfield," she acknowledges; "I love it, because I have lived in it a full and delightful life. . . . I have talked, face to face, with what I reverence; with what I delight in,—with an original, a vigorous, an expanded mind. I have known you, Mr. Rochester" (*Jane Eyre*, chap. 23). Lucy Snowe's relation to Monsieur Paul is literally pedagogic, since he becomes her tutor: "His mind was indeed my library, and whenever it was opened to me, I entered bliss" (*Villette*, chap. 33). Charlotte Brontë, pupil of Monsieur Héger, knew what it was like to be in love with the master, and in her novels she charges the pedagogic relationships with a passion which, though she apparently did not notice it in Jane Austen's novels, she might well have found there in a refined but still intense form.

George Eliot too examined "how potent in us is the infused action of another soul, before which we bow in complete love" (*Daniel Deronda*, chap. 65); but her treatment of the pedagogic relationship differs from Charlotte Brontë's in that it introduces an element of grim irony. Perhaps she remembered with some qualms of embarrassment her adolescent susceptibility to handsome language teachers and elderly pedants[5] and sought to exorcise the memories. Maggie Tulliver begs Philip Wakem, "Teach me everything—wouldn't you? Greek and everything?" (*The Mill on the Floss*, II, chap. 6), and he does undertake to develop her and direct her reading, falling deeply in love with her in the process; but her love for him is a thin cerebral quantity that cannot match the force of her strong sexual attraction to Stephen Guest.

Dorothea Brooke looks joyfully forward to a marriage in which "she would be allowed to live continually in the light of a mind that she could reverence," but finds that Mr. Casaubon's mind is only a series of dark "vaults where he walked taper in hand" (*Middlemarch*, I, chaps. 5, 10). And Gwendolen Harleth, eager to receive Deronda's instruction and render herself in return, discovers that though he is ready enough with the instruction, he doesn't want *her*.

Henry James goes further still in exploring the sinister implications in the pedagogic relationship. That it fascinated him is testified by his first novel, which is about a man who brings up his ward, educates her, and marries her at last. But he leads us through a series of disturbing speculations about the right of one mind to govern another: Maisie is used for dubious purposes in the sexual relations of her parents and parent-surrogates; Miles and Flora apparently either pervert or are perverted by their governess; and Isabel Archer negates herself by trying to conform to the aesthetic standards of the manipulators who surround her. The culmination is the horrible premise of the narrator of *The Sacred Fount*, that what one gives—of youth, of wisdom, of joy—is by definition no longer one's own: that the donor becomes, in the process of giving, correspondingly depleted. You can't eat your cake and have it too. When he hears of how much grace and intelligence a certain lady has imparted to a man, he asks incredulously, "She keeps her wit then, . . . in spite of all she pumps into others?" (chap. 1). And he gradually persuades his interlocutor,

> "Whoever she is, she gives all she has. She keeps nothing back—nothing for herself."
>
> "I see—because *he* takes everything. He just cleans her out." (chap. 3)

Similar metaphors are multiplied, until the one who gives is seen as a "victim," the one who receives as "the author of the sacrifice," and we are presented with a complete theory of human relations as a system of parasitism, of society as composed of vampires and victims. The narrator of *The Sacred Fount* may be a crazy hypothesizer, but James gives his theory a certain authority when he returns to the giving and taking relation again in *The Ambassadors*, where it is hard to resist the conclusion that Chad Newsome has grown fat and sleek while Madame de Vionnet has dwindled to a diaphanous wraith.

Such a progression suggests why Lionel Trilling notes that "the idea of a love based in pedagogy may seem quaint to some modern readers and repellent to others." But he goes on: "unquestionably it plays a decisive part in the power and charm of Jane Austen's art" (*Sincerity and Authenticity*, p. 82). What to James is suspect and potentially horrible, for Jane Austen is a source of power and charm. For her the pedagogic relationship is not parasitic but symbiotic, a relationship that is mutual and joyful: it blesseth him that gives and him that takes. The happy resolutions of her novels celebrate the achieved integration of head and heart that is represented by the pupil and teacher coming to loving accord. Novelists of more tragic vision are unable to visualise so complete a reconciliation. A recurring pattern in the novels of the Brontës, George Eliot, Hardy, Lawrence and others shows a split between the intellectual and the passionate, the Apollonian and the Dionysian, the spiritual and the physical; and the task of the central character is to choose *between* alternatives—between Edgar Linton and Heathcliff, St. John Rivers and Mr. Rochester, Philip Wakem and Stephen Guest, Angel Clare and Alec D'Urberville, Hermione Roddice and Ursula Brangwen. The final choice may be too difficult, and Cathy, Maggie and Tess are destroyed in the process of making it; but even where the choice is made and a fortunate resolution achieved, some loss is implied in the rejected alternative.

The alternative men for the Austen heroine—Wickham, Crawford, Churchill et al.—are far from presenting the same agonizing choice of alternatives. Her feelings for them—if aroused at all, which is doubtful—are transitory and swiftly recognized as a delusion. She generally recognizes joyfully that "We needs must love the highest when we see it,/Not Lancelot, nor another"—and without having to go through the extent of Guinevere's pain and error in the process. The union of Fanny Price with Edmund, say, is entire and satisfying because Edmund has not only "formed her mind" but also "gained her affections" (*MP*, 64), and at the same time.

Richard Simpson, in his fine early study of Jane Austen, pointed out her commitment to "the Platonic idea that the giving and receiving of knowledge . . . is the truest and strongest foundation of love." But he goes on to suggest that this love between her heroes and heroines doesn't amount to much: "Friendship, to judge from her novels, was enough for her; she did not want to exaggerate it into passionate love."[6] Strongly as he is convinced of her merits, he seems to agree with Charlotte Brontë that the stormy sisterhood of the passions have no place in her work[7] and that she opts for esteem rather than passion as the basis of a successful marriage. But Jane Austen will not accept that division—for her the full and mutual engagement of head and heart is what *is* passionate; and any substitute, like Marianne's love for Willoughby, is not only founded on a delusion, but a delusion in itself.

The pattern, however, is of course far more varied than this simplification suggests. Ian Watt observes that Jane Austen's heroines marry older men—"comprehensive epitomes of the Augustan norms such as Mr. Darcy and Mr. Knightley. Her novels in fact dramatize the process whereby feminine and adolescent values are painfully educated in the norms of the mature, rational and educated male world."[8] I don't think one needs to be a woman to recognize that as a dangerous generalization. Elizabeth teaches Darcy as much as he teaches her; Anne and Fanny, in the main course of the novels' action, remain morally static while Wentworth and Edmund get the painful education; and Marianne, though she certainly has plenty to learn, learns from her sister.

That leaves Catherine and Emma, who do get educated in the norms of their men; but even they have a certain power whereby their Pygmalions find that Galatea has turned the tables on them.

Characteristically enough, Jane Austen starts out by being ironic, even satiric, on a theme that she continues to develop through the whole body of her novels. In walking with the Tilneys, Catherine Morland discovers her ignorance on the subject of landscape and the picturesque: "She was heartily ashamed of her ignorance. A misplaced shame. Where people wish to attach, they should always be ignorant. To come with a well-informed mind, is to come with an inability of administering to the vanity of others, which a sensible person would always wish to avoid. A woman especially, if she have the misfortune of knowing any thing, should conceal it as well as she can" (*NA*, 110-111). And the narrator proceeds with an aphoristic discussion of how, though some men will be content with mere ignorance in a woman, most will be satisfied with nothing less than imbecility. Such satire leaves Catherine comparatively unscathed; it is Tilney who needs his vanity administering to.

The satire on the pedagogic relation notwithstanding, Jane Austen goes on to study its operation in realistic terms, and sympathetically: "In the present instance, she confessed and lamented her want of knowledge; . . . and a lecture on the picturesque immediately followed, in which his instructions were so clear that she soon began to see beauty in every thing admired by him, and her attention was so earnest, that he became perfectly satisfied of her having a great deal of natural taste" (111). He sounds like Emma, concluding of Harriet that she is "so grateful for being admitted to Hartfield, and so artlessly impressed by the appearance of everything in so superior a style to what she had been used to, that she must have good sense and deserve encouragement" (*E*, 23). Jane Austen was perfectly aware of the element of self-love in the pedagogic relationship, as was Swift:

> What he had planted, now was grown;
> His Virtues she might call her own.
>
> . . .
>
> Self-love, in Nature rooted fast,
> Attends us first, and leaves us last:
> Why she likes him, admire not at her,
> She loves her self, and that's the matter.
>
> "Cadenus and Vanessa"

Tilney is a kind of god to Catherine—"it was no effort to Catherine to believe that Henry Tilney could never be wrong" (114); but the creature has a concomitant power over her creator, as we find in numbers of such incidents as his dance with her, during which she "enjoyed her usual happiness with Henry Tilney, listening with sparkling eyes to every thing he said; and, in finding him irresistible, becoming so herself" (131). Tilney may well find that "a teachableness of disposition in a young lady is a great blessing" (174).

And, unlike Emma with Harriet, he does have much to teach her, and she duly benefits from his instruction. His insistence on precision with language, as Stuart Tave suggests,[9] teaches her not only to have the right word by which to express herself, but also to define and refine the sentiment that is to be expressed. Like Henry Higgins, to some extent he creates a new identity for her by giving her a new language. And if novel readers are disposed to be disappointed, as Jane Austen predicted, "that his affection originated in nothing better than gratitude" (243), that he loves her only because she has made it so plain that she loves him, we may be consoled to reflect that Tilney needs Catherine just as she needs him, though of course not as much as she needs him. She can't lecture him or consciously re-form him; but she can recognize that "he indulged himself a little too much with the foibles of others" (29)—an indulgence we later see more dangerously practised by Mr. Bennet. And in fact Tilney is not much to be admired in drawing out the absurdities of Mrs. Allen. However just his ridicule of affectation, however minute his discriminations, he is occasionally on the verge of becoming a rather glib satirist, what Isabella Thorpe would egregiously call a "quiz." He is captivated by Catherine's fresh responses and quickly engaged feelings, so that when, like Miranda looking on the brave new world, she exclaims, "Oh! who can ever be tired of Bath?" he answers with genuine appreciation, "Not those who bring such fresh feelings of every sort to it, as you do" (79). Charmingly disenchanted as he is, he needs those fresh feelings, and responds to them.

Nevertheless we are not again to find in Jane Austen's novels so apt and so docile a pupil as Catherine Morland. To move from *Northanger Abbey* to *Pride and Prejudice* is like turning from *The Taming of the Shrew* to *Much Ado*. Henry Tilney and Petruchio have it all, or nearly all, their own way, and have comparatively little to learn from their two Catherines; but between Elizabeth and Darcy, as between Beatrice and Benedick, matters are more evenly balanced. They are both student-teachers; not that either deliberately sets out to instruct or to learn from the other, but they do very resoundingly teach each other a lesson. And, again as with Beatrice and Benedick, the state that exists between them is war: "They never meet but there's a skirmish of wit between them" (I, i).

The similarity between these two gayest of their authors' works sometimes tempts me to speculate whether Jane Austen was consciously following Shakespeare's play.[10] Beatrice, "born in a merry hour" (II, i) is surely kin to Elizabeth, who "dearly love[s] a laugh" (*PP*, 57), and her comment "I was born to speak all mirth and no matter" (II, i) seems echoed in Jane Austen's playful assertion that her novel was "rather too light, and bright, and sparkling; . . . it wants to be stretched out here and there with a long chapter of sense, if it could be had" (*Letters*, 299).

The analogy is pertinent not only for suggesting the exuberant quality of both works, but for illuminating the sexual piquancy of the love-war relation that gives such delightful force and suggestiveness to works like *The Rape of the Lock*, *Pamela*, *Jane Eyre*, or the wife of Bath's prologue and tale. The stream of criticism that contends the old maid Miss Austen wrote sexless novels seems to me thoroughly imperceptive.[11] Elizabeth's physical vitality, expressing itself in her running, her "jumping over stiles and springing over puddles" (32), is a sexual vitality too; and Darcy's strongly sexual response to her, as he gradually succumbs to her "fine eyes," is quite sufficiently dramatized. We see in Elizabeth as in Beatrice the subsumed attraction that is behind their antagonism; although they always fight with their men, they are always thinking of them. Beatrice, separated as she thinks from Benedick in the masked dance, says almost wistfully, "I would he had boarded me"; and Elizabeth can't see Miss de Bourgh without reflecting, "She looks sickly and cross.—Yes, she will do for him very well" (158)—the "him" in her consciousness being Darcy—nor be introduced to Lady Catherine without searching her countenance for a resemblance to her nephew (162)—always a tell-tale sign. But relations between her and Darcy proceed stormily: she refuses to dance with him, and he is the more attracted. When she does dance with him, she quarrels with him about Wickham. They spar in the dance, skirmish at the piano, fence in conversation. Beatrice's sallies on "Signior Mountanto" are echoed in Elizabeth's witticisms at Darcy's expense: "I am perfectly convinced . . . that Mr. Darcy has no defect. He owns it himself without disguise" (57). Such is their "merry war"—very provocative, very delightful.

But the battles are not love play only; they have their serious issues in which, without usually intending it, the antagonists set up their standards for the other to conform to or reject. Elizabeth is initially closest to being the pedagogue. Bingley recognizes her as "a studier of character" (42); and in admitting "Follies and nonsense, whims and inconsistencies *do* divert me, I own, and I laugh at them whenever I can" (57), she achieves the status of a kind of licensed satirist during her brief stay at Netherfield. She makes full use of that license in her critical analyses of character. In a playful context, she is a teacher catechising a potential student in order to place him:

> "Follies and nonsense, . . . I suppose, are precisely what you are without."
> "Perhaps that is not possible for any one [replies Darcy]. But it has been the study of my life to avoid those weaknesses which often expose a strong understanding to ridicule."
> "Such as vanity and pride."
> "Yes, vanity is a weakness indeed. But pride—where there is a real superiority of mind, pride will be always under good regulation."
> Elizabeth turned away to hide a smile.
> "Your examination of Mr. Darcy is over, I presume," said Miss Bingley;—"and pray what is the result?" (57)

"The study of my life," "real superiority of mind," "good regulation," "examination"—this is classroom terminology. And though Darcy goes through this play catechism with the smiling detachment of an adult who has already done with exams, he is to recall and eventually be changed by Elizabeth's standards as implied in these dialogues. There are three main subjects on which Elizabeth "examines" him in the course of the novel and in which he acquits himself with varying degrees of credit, at various attempts.

The first issue is his right of influence over Bingley, canvassed at length in a Netherfield discussion complete with a hypothetical case, as in an exam question (48-51). Ironically Elizabeth, who is far from being an infallible teacher, takes the opposite side in this argument from that she is to take in practice afterwards, here she defends Bingley's "merit" in his readiness "to yield readily—easily—to the *persuasion* of a friend" (50), whereas later she is to be indignant that Darcy makes him do just that.

The second aspect of Darcy's character that Elizabeth probes at Netherfield is what she calls, when he admits "my good opinion once lost is lost forever," his "implacable resentment" (58). Here the practical test Elizabeth administers is Wickham, against whom she believes that that resentment has been unjustly vented. Unjustifiable influence over his friend and brutal persecution of his enemy: these are the two offences she accuses Darcy of in the first proposal scene. She has examined him as a candidate for her hand and she fails him resoundingly. Having failed the viva voce, Darcy voluntarily sits a written exam—his letter—not to qualify himself for the same position, but to justify himself as a man of right conduct. This paper is enough to teach the teacher how wrong she has been, how "blind, partial, prejudiced, absurd."

> "How despicably have I acted!" she cried.—"I, who have prided myself on my discernment!—I, who have valued myself on my abilities! . . . I have courted prepossession and ignorance, and driven reason away, where either were concerned. Till this moment, I never knew myself." (208)

It is a salutary lesson for one who has been more fond of detecting shortcomings in others than in herself.

Darcy is to be further exonerated from the charge of implacable resentment by his remarkably forbearing behavior to Elizabeth herself, who certainly gives provocation for resentment: after she quarrels with him in the dance, his feelings for her "soon procured her pardon" (94); and though his letter after her insulting refusal begins in bitterness, "the adieu is charity itself" (368). He has been tested by having had a lot to put up with, and he has been admirably tolerant and forgiving.

However, in the third issue Darcy has more to learn and does not acquit himself creditably until the last part of the novel. It is not a question of conduct or principle but of manners. Again the matter is playfully canvassed between them in conversation—as usual, with an audience at hand—this time at the piano at Rosings. Elizabeth threatens to tell Colonel Fitzwilliam of Darcy's misdemeanours in Hertfordshire:

> "You shall hear then—but prepare yourself for something

> very dreadful. The first time of my ever seeing him in Hertfordshire, you must know, was at a ball—and at this ball, what do you think he did? He danced only four dances! I am sorry to pain you—but so it was. He danced only four dances, though gentlemen were scarce; and, to my certain knowledge, more than one young lady was sitting down in want of a partner. Mr. Darcy, you cannot deny the fact. . . ."
>
> "I certainly have not the talent which some people possess," said Darcy, "of conversing easily with those I have never seen before. I cannot catch their tone of conversation, or appear interested in their concerns, as I often see done."
>
> "My fingers," said Elizabeth, "do not move over this instrument in the masterly manner which I see so many women's do. They have not the same force or rapidity, and do not produce the same expression. But then I have always supposed it to be my own fault—because I would not take the trouble of practicing. It is not that I do not believe *my* fingers as capable as any other woman's of superior execution." (175)

Elizabeth's shortcomings as pedagogue are still apparent in the continuing operation of that initial incident at the Meryton assembly that wounded her vanity, but here in essence she is right. Her analogy is apt: she lets Darcy know that gracious manners are not acquired simply as a ready-made gift from heaven but that they are a skill to be developed like other skills by exertion and practice. But Darcy, though he accepts her analogy, misapplies it and so doesn't profit from her instruction: "You are perfectly right," he acknowledges; "No one admitted to the privilege of hearing you, can think any thing wanting. We neither of us perform to strangers" (176). But piano-playing is an accomplishment that anyone may choose or not choose to develop; gracious manners are a duty that everyone must practice, and most particularly those with Darcy's prominent position in the world. Again, it takes a practical issue to make the point. Darcy's churlish first proposal brings a fierce rebuke which this time sinks in, so that he can even quote it months afterwards: "Your reproof, so well applied, I shall never forget: 'had you behaved in a more gentleman-like manner.' Those were your words" (367). In the interval, like a good pupil, he has made a conscious effort "to correct my temper," and he displays his newly acquired skill when they meet at Pemberley; as he tells her afterwards: " 'My object *then* . . . was to shew you, by every civility in my power, that I was not so mean as to resent the past; and I hoped to obtain your forgiveness, to lessen your ill opinion, by letting you see that your reproofs had been attended to.' " (370). In this matter he has acknowledged his shortcomings and studied to correct them: "You taught me a lesson," he acknowledges fervently (369). Like Benedick, he has resolved, "I must not seem proud. Happy are they that hear their detractions and can put them to mending" (II, iii).

Elizabeth has had plenty to learn too, but Darcy, though he is the occasion of her increased self-knowledge, is not so clearly the agent. The theoretical discussions at Netherfield and Rosings, which are subsequently so neatly put to the test, are about Darcy's behaviour, not Elizabeth's. Hers have been the faults of the examiner who has overestimated her qualifications and totally misjudged her examinees. They are faults not of conduct but of judgment, so that in the process whereby her failing candidate proves himself eminently qualified, and her favoured student does the reverse, she has come to know her shortcomings and herself.

In the question of Wickham's wrongs and Darcy's supposedly implacable resentment, she was entirely misguided, and Darcy had no fault to correct; and in the first issue discussed between them, his influence on Bingley, she has learned that it is wrong only if exerted in the wrong direction; she ceases to be fanatical in her views here, but it is an issue that will arise again for playful debate between them. Darcy does still unblushingly keep Bingley under strict if friendly surveillance, and Bingley dares propose to Jane only with Darcy's permission: "Elizabeth longed to observe that Mr. Bingley had been a most delightful friend; so easily guided that his worth was invaluable; but she checked herself. She remembered that he had yet to learn to be laughed at, and it was rather too early to begin" (371). That is a charming little preview of their marriage, confirming Elizabeth's earlier discovery that "It was an union that must have been to the advantage of both; by her ease and liveliness, his mind might have been softened, his manners improved, and from his judgment, information, and knowledge of the world, she must have received benefit of greater importance" (312). Elizabeth by the time they are engaged has learned some tact and forbearance in the exercise of her wit; and Darcy, having learned manners, must go on learning—he must learn to be laughed at.

In *Pride and Prejudice* we see the pedagogic relationship stormily in process; in *Mansfield Park* it is virtually a fait accompli by the time the main action of the novel begins. By the end of the second chapter we get a summary of Edmund's central role in Fanny's education and her response:

> His attentions were . . . of the highest importance in assisting the improvement of her mind, and extending its pleasures. He knew her to be clever, to have a quick apprehension as well as good sense. . . . He recommended the books which charmed her leisure hours, he encouraged her taste, and corrected her judgment. . . . In return for such services she loved him better than anybody in the world except William; her heart was divided between the two. (22)

By his early pedagogic role he has "formed her mind and gained her affections" (64). Fanny's story is to begin when, as the now qualified star pupil, she watches her honoured master stray into error and pain, led there by her rival, the wayward pupil. What she has learned is put to its severest test when she must detach the learning from the tutor and subject him to the tests of the very principles he has taught her.

It is noteworthy that Fanny feels her "first actual pain" when Edmund adopts the pedagogic stance with Mary—he teaches her to ride. His instructions to Fanny have always had a strongly moral cast: "You are sorry to leave Mamma, my dear little Fanny," he once comforted her, "which shows you to be a very good girl" (15); to maintain that role of the good girl in Edmund's estimation becomes her constant practice. But to Mary Crawford, whose attractions are more overtly physical, he initially teaches a physical activity. When Fanny, neglected and sorry for herself, watches from afar, she has cause to feel a pang at the physical intimacy that his instruction promotes: "After a few minutes, they stopt entirely, Edmund was close to her, he was speaking to her, he was evidently directing her management of the bridle, he had hold of her hand; she saw it, or the imagination supplied what the eye could not reach" (67). Fanny as a child had her own feelings warmed by such attention from Edmund, when he ruled her lines for her letters and stood by "to assist her with his penknife or his orthography, as either were wanted" (16). Now she is naturally quick to discover Edmund's attraction to his new pupil, and he is soon making her his confidante in his discussion of the shortcomings and charms of her rival.

> "I am glad you saw it all as I did" [he tells her after one such discussion].
>
> Having formed her mind and gained her affections, he had a good chance of her thinking like him; though at this period, and on this subject, there began now to be some danger of dissimilarity, for he was in a line of admiration of Miss Crawford, which might lead him where Fanny could not follow. (64)

It is in this direction that Fanny's story is to develop. She has been and is a good pupil, and the love that grew out of the pedagogic relation is to remain constant; but Fanny is to graduate from the status of pupil to adult in the process of separating her judgment from Edmund's and detecting him in error. Fanny as pupil "regarded her cousin as an example of every thing good and great. . . . Her sentiments towards him were compounded of all that was respectful, grateful, confiding, and tender" (37). Fanny as adolescent wonders, "Could it be possible? Edmund so inconsistent. . . . Was he not wrong?" (156). Fanny as adult discovers, "He is blinded, and nothing will open his eyes" (424). But the pupil is morally debarred from opening her master's eyes, even though he recognizes her sound judgment and even reverses their roles by applying to her for advice: she cannot in honour denigrate her rival; hence her story must be a "trial," like Pamela's or the Duchess of Malfi's; and like Jane Austen's other actively passive heroines, Elinor and Anne, she must achieve through endurance rather than through action.

Mary Crawford, though she outclasses Fanny as a horsewoman, proves to be morally a totally intractable pupil. Edmund's most sustained effort in instructing her is the conversation in the wood at Sotherton, where he carefully justifies his decision to enter the ministry and persuasively explains the importance of a clergyman's duties. His lecture elicits an earnest "Certainly" from Fanny, but Mary Crawford asserts, "I am just as much surprised now as I was at first that you should intend to take orders" (93). She is simply determined not to listen; her mind is closed. And her very recalcitrance has its attractions for the teacher, who begins to succumb to that danger, not unknown to many of us, of paying most attention to the worst students: "He still reasoned with her, but in vain. She would not calculate, she would not compare. She would only smile and assert. The greatest degree of rational consistency could not have been more engaging, and they talked with mutual satisfaction" (96). Committing another familiar fault of pedagogues, he excuses her shortcomings as a moral student by blaming her previous educators: "Yes, that uncle and aunt! They have injured the finest mind!" (269).

Though Mary closes her mind to Edmund's influence, she is ambitious to influence *him*. In her case it is not that her chief end is his moral welfare, but that she enjoys power. When she urges him to go into law (93) she could conceivably have his good, as well as her own, in view; but in the matter of the play her tactics in persuading him to take the part of Anhalt are directed not only to getting him to play opposite her, but also simply to conquering him, because she relishes the triumph of making him act against his principles. Her fondest memory is of this victory: "His sturdy spirit to bend as it did! Oh, it was sweet beyond all expression" (358). This sinister bit of gloating is another of the touches that remind us of Mary as temptress, seductress—as even Satanic.

Lovers' Vows provides a paradigm for the novel in that Edmund's role is Anhalt, who is literally the tutor of the heroine, Amelia. There are some crude statements there of themes Jane Austen enlarges on more subtly in the novel. Amelia tells her tutor, for instance, "My father has more than once told me that he who forms my mind I should always consider as my greatest benefactor. (*looking down*) And my heart tells me the same" (503-504).[12] And when Anhalt admits that "love" is the subject of their discourse, Amelia pursues, "(*going up to him*). Come, then, teach it me—teach it me as you taught me geography, languages, and other important things" (506). Such might well be Fanny's sentiments, though of course she would never voice them. But it is Mary who plays Amelia's part: Mary has Amelia's brass and Amelia's sense that her tutor is her social inferior, a sense that ultimately makes her unable to accept Edmund. But Fanny has been the docile and loving pupil, and it is notable that both Edmund and Mary feel the need to rehearse their parts in Fanny's presence. Amelia's role of the enamoured pupil combines Edmund's two women.

Emma, like Mary Crawford, is a bad pupil. They both have the talents to be good students but the temperament to resist instruction. But though that is the whole of Mary's story, it is only a part of Emma's.

The novel opens on the evening of Miss Taylor's withdrawal from Hartfield and Mr. Knightley's consequent friendly visit. Miss Taylor, we hear at the outset, has long been Emma's friend rather than her governess; and Emma though "highly esteeming Miss Taylor's judgment . . . [has been] directed chiefly by her own" (*E*, 5). Mr. Knightley is to tell her affectionately that she is "very fit for a wife, but not at all for a governess" (38). Still, she has been there, and now she has gone. That scene introduces not only the marriage theme of the novel and "the question of independence or dependence,"[13] but also the theme of Emma's education. Exit governess, enter governor: "Mr. Knightley, in fact, was one of the few people who could see faults in Emma Woodhouse, and the only one who ever told her of them: . . . this was not particularly agreeable to Emma herself" (11). That is the initial situation, which we see dramatized at length in subsequent scenes. Emma doesn't like to be told she has anything to learn, and she argues.

On nearly all the questions at issue between them—and the working of these constitutes the novel's structure—Mr. Knightley is right and Emma is wrong. Mr. Knightley condemns her matchmaking propensity: "Your time has been properly and delicately spent," he says with sarcasm, "if you have been endeavouring for the last four years to bring about this marriage" (12). But Emma insists, "Only one more [match]; . . . only for Mr. Elton" (13). And at the end she realizes how "with unpardonable arrogance [she had] proposed to arrange everybody's destiny" (413). Mr. Knightley objects to Emma's intimacy with Harriet, whom he calls "the very worst sort of companion that Emma could possibly have" (38). Emma maintains the intimacy notwithstanding but is to exclaim at last, "Oh God! that I had never seen her!" (411). Mr. Knightley wants her to recognize Jane Fairfax's better claims to attention, but Emma persists in neglecting her, until she is made aware of her "past injustice towards Miss Fairfax" (421). Mr. Knightley tells her she is not sufficiently considerate towards Miss Bates; but his hints are not "equal to counteract the persuasion of its being very disagreeable" (155), until she eventually reproaches herself bitterly, "How could she have been so brutal, so cruel to Miss Bates!" (376). The only matter on which Mr. Knightley's judgment is not fully to be trusted is the merits, or lack of them, of Frank Churchill, and here Emma is shrewd:

> "You seem determined to think ill of him."
> "Me!—not at all," replied Mr. Knightley, rather displeased. (149)

His jealousy, quite forgivably, is the only passion that will lead his otherwise sound judgment astray.

So, as in *Pride and Prejudice*, there is the beautifully symmetrical pattern of the precept laid down and discussed in theory, the practical test, and the access of knowledge with experience. Emma is the wayward pupil; she does not simply close her mind like Mary Crawford, but she refuses to acknowledge she has anything to learn for as long as she can. And there is a focus of emotional intensity in the arguments, in Mr. Knightley's pleasure when Emma seems to have taken his advice, in his disappointment when she turns out to be unreformed; in Emma's fluctuations between rebelliousness and fear of his "tall indignation" (60), and in her schemes for placating him without actually taking his advice. In the scene where he exclaims, "Nonsense, errant nonsense, as ever was talked!" to her argument that Robert Martin is not fit for Harriet,

> Emma made no answer, and tried to look cheerfully unconcerned, but was really feeling uncomfortable and wanting him very much to be gone. She did not repent what she had done; she still thought herself a better judge of such a point of female right and refinement than he could be; yet she had a sort of habitual respect for his judgment in general, which made her dislike having it so loudly against her; and to have him sitting just opposite to her in angry state, was very disagreeable. (65)

Like other wayward pupils who would rather resort to wiles

than learn the lesson, she contrives a reconciliation with him while they are in physical contact, dandling their mutual niece. "It did assist; for though he began with grave looks and short questions, he was soon led on to . . . take the child out of her arms with all the unceremoniousness of perfect amity" (98).

On another occasion she plays with his eagerness that she should properly appreciate Jane Fairfax. He warmly praises her attentions as hostess; "I am happy you approved," she says, smiling; but deliberately adds her old objection, "Miss Fairfax is reserved" (170-171).

> "My dear Emma," said he, moving from his chair into one close by her, "you are not going to tell me, I hope, that you had not a pleasant evening."
>
> "Oh! no; I was pleased with my own perseverance in asking questions, and amused to think how little information I obtained."
>
> "I am disappointed," was his only answer. . . .
>
> Emma saw his anxiety, and wishing to appease it, at least for the present, said, and with a sincerity which no one could question–
>
> "She is a sort of elegant creature that one cannot keep one's eyes from. I am always watching her to admire; and I do pity her from my heart."
>
> Mr. Knightley looked as if he were more gratified than he cared to express. (171)

Here we trace the emotions of the pedagogue, eager for his student's progress: his warm physical approach, his distress in her backsliding, his gratification in the appeasement.

Emma as rebellious student often tries to bring Mr. Knightley round to her way of thinking, and occasionally has the pedagogue's pleasure in success. When he acknowledges Harriet's claims by dancing with her after Mr. Elton's slight, Emma is jubilant. "Never had she been more surprised, seldom more delighted, than at that instant. She was all pleasure and gratitude, . . . and longed to be thanking him; and though too distant for speech, her countenance said much, as soon as she could catch his eye again" (328). Even here, where Emma is delighting in his attention to her own star pupil, we are reminded of her subconscious love by a hint of jealousy: "Harriet would have seemed almost too lucky, if it had not been for the cruel state of things before" (328).

The culmination of all these arguments, the pedagogic battles and the latent love, is of course the Miss Bates incident. It is the emotional climax of the novel. Mr. Knightley believes Emma will very soon marry his rival, but for the last time claims his privilege of remonstrating when he sees her acting wrongly. "Emma recollected, blushed, was sorry, but tried to laugh it off" (374)–the usual pattern. He persists in his reproach, however, and this time he gets to her: "she felt it at her heart" (376). But there is no time for placation or reconciliation, and after the hurried parting, Emma is utterly desolate. All her confidence in her own judgment, her perserverance in her own courses, her determination not to give in, are done away with. She mends her ways and calls on Miss Bates, rather hoping Mr. Knightley will find her so creditably occupied: "She had no objection. She would not be ashamed of the appearance of the penitence, so justly and truly hers" (377-378). She is a new Emma. And when Mr. Knightley does understand that she has learned his lesson and is not resentful, it is a moment of full and loving accord, and physically expressed: "He looked at her with a glow of regard. . . . He took her hand;– whether she had not herself made the first motion, she could not say–she might, perhaps, have rather offered it–but he took her hand, pressed it, and certainly was on the point of carrying it to his lips" (385-386). Emma and Mr. Knightley have both more to learn about each other's feelings before that kiss can happen; but that spontaneous and simultaneous clasp of the hands, in the moment of harmony between master and pupil, is a memorable image for the mutually passionate and joyful commitment implied in the pedagogic relationship in Jane Austen's novels.

Emma's and Mr. Knightley's love has grown and been manifested in their relations as master and pupil. When Emma discovers her love for him, it is in terms of his teaching role: "He had loved her, and watched over her from a girl, with an endeavour to improve her, and an anxiety for her doing right, which no other creature had at all shared" (415); and when he avows his love for her, it is in the same terms: "You hear nothing but truth from me.–I have blamed you, and lectured you, and you have borne it as no other woman in England would have borne it" (430). Mind and heart have been fully and simultaneously involved so that the love has found its existence and expression through the teaching and the learning. In Mr. Knightley's case, by his own avowal, it is the love that has taken precedence of the education: "My interference was quite as likely to do harm as good. . . . The good was all to myself, by making you an object of the tenderest affection to me" (462).

In *Persuasion* it is the hero who must learn, while the heroine remains morally static. But we do not have a full reversal of the Emma-Mr. Knightley situation, in that Anne teaches Wentworth not by precept but by example, so that she doesn't really qualify for the pedagogue's role in that relation. As in *Pride and Prejudice*, the principals of this novel are in a sense antagonists–Wentworth is determined to stay angry with Anne as Elizabeth is determined to dislike Darcy–but here we have no merry war. The "perpetual estrangement" (64) is a cause not of merriment but of pain and gives the novel its emotional poignancy. Anne is isolated from the man she loves and can neither influence nor be influenced by him for much of the novel. This estrangement is emphasized by the fact that hero and heroine briefly and abortively set up pedagogic relations elsewhere.

Wentworth takes on the role of pedagogue for his other woman and, being offended by Anne's persuasibility, lectures Louisa on the virtues of firmness: "My first wish for all, whom I am interested in, is that they should be firm" (88). The misguided teacher finds an enthusiastic pupil, and Louisa, "being now armed with the idea of merit in maintaining her own way" (94), insists on going to Lyme, insists on being jumped from stiles, insists on leaping from the Cobb. "I am determined I will," she declares (109), and so she comes a cropper.

In the interval Anne has become instructress for another man too, the bereaved Captain Benwick, who like her is grieving over a lost love. She gives him a bracing lecture on fortitude, and, "feeling in herself the right of seniority of mind," directs him to read "such works of our best moralists . . . as occurred to her at the moment as calculated to rouse and fortify the mind by the highest precepts" (101). She is not without a wry sense of the irony of her role as instructress: "Anne could not but be amused at the idea of her coming to Lyme, to preach patience and resignation to a young man whom she had never seen before; nor could she help fearing, on more serious reflection, that, like many other great moralists and preachers, she had been eloquent on a point in which her own conduct would ill bear examination" (101). For all this, Benwick responds as warmly to her instructions as Louisa does to Wentworth's and seems so ready and eager to be consoled that he is in a fair way to forgetting his lost fiancée in falling in love with Anne.

However, by that symmetrical recoupling caused by the accident on the Cobb, the two facile pupils are thrown together and very plausibly united, so clearing away at least some of the obstacles between their instructors. Anne "saw no reason against their being happy. . . . They would soon grow more alike. He would gain cheerfulness, and she would learn to be an enthusiast for Scott and Lord Byron; nay, that was probably learnt already; of course they had fallen in love over poetry" (167). There is a little history in miniature of a pedagogic relationship, stripped of the perils and pitfalls encountered by more complex souls like Elizabeth, Darcy and Emma.

Anne has not been Wentworth's instructress, except indirectly in the scene where he overhears her fervent speech on constancy; but she has been the occasion of his learning. He tells her how at Lyme he had "received lessons of more than one sort. . . . There, he had learnt to distinguish between the steadiness of principle and the obstinacy of self-will" (242). Anne is more fortunate than many a teacher in being able to claim, "I must believe that I was right, much as I suffered from it" (246). But Wentworth, like Darcy who must learn to be laughed at, is to continue his education: "I must learn to brook being happier than I deserve" (247). It is a propitious ending.

Jane Austen has greater faith than most writers in the love fully combined with knowledge of self and esteem for the partner that is implied in her version of the pedagogic relationship. That mutual contribution to the formation of character, that mingling of minds as well as hearts and bodies, is joyful and totally fulfilling. But in Jane Austen there is always a qualification. I have been talking about the pedagogic relationship in its successful operation, as it occurs between hero and heroine, with its emotional and sexual implications. But it is not always successful. And like Henry James, Jane Austen examines with a critical eye both the right of one mind to influence another, and the complicity of the mind that allows itself to be influenced. She is fully aware of the possible arrogance of the pedagogic enterprise between fallible human beings: we need only remember Emma and Harriet. She occasionally endorses Elizabeth's touch of cynicism (it is before Elizabeth learns that she had indeed taught Darcy a lesson): "We all love to instruct, though we can teach only what is not worth knowing" (*PP*, 343). And she gives full attention to the mischief done by misguided mentors, however well intentioned, like Sir Thomas and Mrs. Norris, and finally says of the original Persuader, "There was nothing less for Lady Russell to do, than to admit that she had been pretty completely wrong, and to take up a new set of opinions and of hopes" (*P*, 249).

Persuasion is an issue not only in the last novel. Darcy's control of Bingley, Emma's of Harriet, Mary's of Edmund are critically examined, and the principals are judged as arrogant, as pliable, as silly, in their different degrees. Ultimately Jane Austen insists that richly as a pupil may receive, or disastrously as he may be misled, he is responsible. He cannot be a mere passive receptacle of wisdom, or a mere victim of bad advice. The pupil makes his choices: he may choose or not choose to be instructed; he may elect his instructor; he may select which of the instructions to attend to. In all these choices he defines himself, and he has himself to accuse if they are wrong. There can be no shrugging off the blame. Emma is blameworthy in her influence on Harriet, and is certainly fortunate that Robert Martin is so manfully persistent as to get Harriet in the end anyway; but then Harriet had no business allowing Emma to run her life for her in the first place; and, had he lost her, Martin's loss would have been so much the less. This issue of responsibility is fully explored in *Mansfield Park*, where Edmund tries to excuse Mary's behaviour by putting the blame on her education and at last extorts Fanny's impatient outburst, "Her friends leading her astray for years! She is quite as likely to have led *them* astray" (424). Jane Fairfax carefully avoids Edmund's kind of injustice in her apology to Mrs. Weston: "Do not imagine, madam, . . . that I was taught wrong. Do not let any reflection fall on the principles or the care of the friends who brought me up. The error has been all my own" (*E*, 419). It is a noble declaration: a brave and full acceptance of responsibility.

Embedded in all Jane Austen's novels is a pedagogic story, a story not just of learning—most novels are that—but of teaching too. We see courses of instruction proceeding through initiation, lectures, examination, graduation, qualification. We hear of pupils apt, too eager, or recalcitrant; of teachers discerning, misguided, or perverse. All this bears much of the moral import of the novels, as the reader learns along with the lecturers and the students. But it also carries the emotional interest, as hero and heroine respond to each other fully and consciously, come to share their experience, their feelings, and themselves, and are thus wholly united. T. S. Eliot would perhaps disclaim the analogy, but it seems to me that the "felt thought" that he finds as the characteristic of metaphysical poetry[14] has some kinship with the "intelligent love" that Lionel Trilling finds as Jane Austen's ideal. She too presents an intense and simultaneous commitment of feeling and intelligence, and her novels within their sphere dramatize the achievement of that commitment. She shows us what is for her the most passionate love, a love that is fully aware. Emma comes to realize that her first endeavour must be "to understand, thoroughly to understand her own heart" (*E*, 412). I have no apologies to make for the spinster Jane, even though she may never show us her lovers in bed. In the fullest sense she understood love, and made sure her best men and women come to do so too.

NOTES

1. The phrase is Pamela Hansford Johnson's in "The Sexual Life in Dickens's Novels," *Dickens 1970*, ed. Michael Slater (London: Chapman and Hall, 1970), p. 179.

2. *Sincerity and Authenticity* (London: Oxford University Press, 1972), p. 82. Trilling has elsewhere sardonically commented, "I know that pedagogy is a depressing subject to all persons of sensibility" ("On the Teaching of Modern Literature," *Beyond Culture* [New York: Viking Press, 1965], p. 3).

3. Geoffrey Gorer has explored this aspect of the novels in "The Myth in Jane Austen," *American Imago*, 2 (1941), 197-204.

4. See, for instance, David Smith, "Incest Patterns in two Victorian Novels," *Literature and Psychology*, 15 (1965), 135-162.

5. See Gordon S. Haight, *George Eliot: A Biography* (London and New York: Oxford University Press, 1968), pp. 27, 49-50.

6. Unsigned review of James Austen-Leigh's *Memoir of Jane Austen* in the *North British Review* (April, 1870). It is readily available in *Jane Austen: the Critical Heritage*, ed. B. C. Southam (London:

Routledge and Kegan Paul, 1968), from which I take my text, pp. 244 and 246.

7. Letter to W. S. Williams, April 12, 1850. *The Shakespeare Head Brontë* (Oxford: Basil Blackwell, 1931-1934), 14:499. See Southam, p. 128.

8. "Serious Reflections on *The Rise of the Novel*," *Novel: A Forum on Fiction*, 1 (1968), 218. Sylvia Myers has already challenged Watt for this characteristic bit of swashbuckling in her article in the same journal, "Womanhood in Jane Austen's Novels," 3 (1970), 225-232.

9. See *Some Words of Jane Austen* (Chicago: University of Chicago Press, 1973), chaps. 1 and 2.

10. One can note a similarity not only in the main plot, where hero and heroine come to accord only after pointedly singling each other out for abuse, but also in the subplots—the making and breaking of the Hero/Claudio and Jane/Bingley matches being a point at fierce issue between the main characters. "God help the noble Claudio! If he have caught the Benedick, it will cost him a thousand pounds ere 'a be cured" (I, i), says Beatrice, and so might Elizabeth say of Bingley and Darcy. Hero's description of Beatrice, who "turns . . . every man the wrong side out" (III, i), sounds like the unreformed Elizabeth: "Disdain and scorn ride sparkling in her eyes, / Misprising what they look on, and her wit / Values itself so highly that to her / All matter else seems weak. She cannot love / . . . She is so self-endeared." And when Beatrice brings herself to love Benedick, she might be Elizabeth soliloquizing after talking to the housekeeper at Pemberley: "For others say thou dost deserve, and I / Believe it better than reportingly" (III, i). Darcy is obviously not so like Benedick. But he too is confident—as well he might be with Miss Bingley and Miss de Bourgh visibly eager to snap him up—that "It is certain I am loved of all ladies, only you excepted" (I, i); and Benedick's determination that "till all graces be in one woman, one woman shall not come in my grace" (II, iii) is echoed in Darcy's exacting notions of what constitutes accomplishment in a woman. When it comes to the point, Benedick, like Darcy, finds it difficult to express himself warmly and captivatingly: "No, I was not born under a rhyming planet, nor I cannot woo in festival terms" (V, ii). Amen to that, Elizabeth at Hunsford might well have agreed!

11. Cf. Lloyd W. Brown: "The myth of the asexual Jane Austen novel is more revealing of our surfeited twentieth-century 'senses'

than it is of Jane Austen's work" ("Jane Austen and the Feminist Tradition," *Nineteenth-Century Fiction*, 28 [1973], 333).

12. I use Chapman's edition of the play, included with his edition of *Mansfield Park*.

13. See Arnold Kettle's section on *Emma* in *An Introduction to the English Novel* (London: Hutchinson University Library, 1951).

14. I refer to his essay of 1921, "The Metaphysical Poets," reprinted in *Collected Essays* (London: Faber and Faber, 1932).

NORMAN PAGE

ORDERS OF MERIT

> But now really, do not you think Udolpho the nicest book in the world?
>
> *Northanger Abbey*

The steady and often slow maturing of a novelist's art, the progression from "early" to "middle" and "late" phases, the distinctive features of individual novels or of one "period" compared with another—these are not matters with which Austen criticism has on the whole been much concerned. For various reasons, questions which have loomed large in the discussion of, say, Dickens or Henry James have often been passed over as of little importance or relevance in connection with Jane Austen. Nor is it difficult to see why this should have been so. The publication of her work covers a mere half-dozen years, compared with Dickens's three-and-a-half decades and James's four; by the standards of *Bleak House* or *The Portrait of a Lady* her novels are all short; the chronology of their composition, and in some cases their palimpsest-like growth through a series of radical rewritings, complicate the issue sufficiently to inhibit easy generalizations about "early" and "late"; and the six novels possess certain common characteristics which it is possible to exaggerate but which nevertheless encourage the tendency to think of them as forming installments, as it were, of a single long work, or, to put it another way, to suppose that Jane Austen wrote what was in essence the same novel over and over again. The validity of these assumptions is not at the moment the point at issue: of course we know that her writing life covers more like thirty years than six, and that the juvenilia are essential to a consideration of her development, which was a genuine and impressive phenomenon; but the attitudes I have indicated have been widespread, and have resulted in her receiving special, and signally inadequate, treatment on many occasions. The narrowness of her social range and settings and what has been taken to be the evenness of her style have no doubt also contributed to the same prejudices and misconceptions; and too many of her critics, until quite recent times, have implicitly assented to the view articulated by W. F. Pollock more than a century ago: "The uniform quality of her work is one most remarkable point to be observed in it. Let a volume be opened at any place: there is the same good English, the same refined style, the same simplicity and truth."[1] A small, compact, homogeneous body of work, capable of being discussed as an entity, in which the recurrence of themes and character types is somehow more significant than the structural and tonal contrasts between novels—this, or something like it, has been the verdict on the novels implied by much of the criticism of the past, though there are of course some distinguished exceptions. Now it is certainly easier to trace common elements between *Northanger Abbey* and *Emma* than between *The Pickwick Papers* and *Great Expectations*, or between *Scenes of Clerical Life* and *Daniel Deronda*. But it seems worth stressing anew the distinctive qualities of Jane Austen's novels, individually considered, as a corrective to the tendency, which they themselves admittedly encourage, to treat them as a set of six variations on a theme.

In one way, it is true, the uniqueness of each one of the novels has been conceded right from the start; and it is worth inquiring into one aspect of their individuality by considering what answers have been given and may be given to the naive but not pointless question: which is Jane Austen's best novel? Insofar as "best" may be interpreted as that which most fully embodies her characteristic strengths, this strategy may appear to do no more than play into the hands of the generalizers, those who stress the similarities rather than the differences between the novels. But to name a particular novel, and still more to make special claims for it, is to grant it independent status; and although the grounds of preference may not always have been formulated, it is possible to make some attempt to deduce them. I propose to treat the question first historically and then judicially: that is to say, to consider what different answers have been made at different times to this question; and then to consider on what grounds one or another answer might be given in our own time. Thus formulated, the question, if crude, is at least manageable; and even such a modest investigation into a single episode in the history of literary taste and judgment may serve to suggest something not only of the development of Jane Austen's reputation but also of the fictional perceptions and blind spots of several generations of readers.

There is enough evidence to indicate that Jane Austen herself was far from indifferent to the assessment of her books, severally regarded and in relation to each other. Apart from scattered references in the surviving letters, that she should have gone to the trouble of collecting and transcribing from a variety of sources the "Opinions" of *Mansfield Park* and *Emma* which exist in her hand implies that she cared about, or at any rate was interested in, the judgments of her readers; and it is a prominent feature of these informal comments that they habitually take the form of comparisons between one novel and another.[2] Moreover, the degree of unanimity is sufficient to strike us, as it must surely have struck the novelist. Fifteen of the collected observations on *Mansfield Park* compare it to *Pride and Prejudice*, and of these a dozen indicate a preference for the latter. A similar situation prevails with respect to *Emma*, *Pride and Prejudice* again emerging as the overwhelming favorite. (Cassandra Austen, whose opinion was perhaps worth more to the author than a heap of others, was exceptional in liking *Mansfield Park* the best of the three, and *Pride and Prejudice* the least, though she did concede that the former was "not so brilliant" as the latter.) The general verdict would hardly have offended the author, for whom *Pride and Prejudice* was "my own darling child" (*Letters*, 297), and there may be some significance in her manner of self-identification on the title pages of the first edition of *Emma* and the second edition of *Mansfield Park* as "the Author of 'Pride and Prejudice.' "

Admiration and sometimes preference for *Pride and Prejudice* was echoed publicly and privately by many other nineteenth-century readers, including such diverse judges as Sheridan, William Gifford, Miss Mitford, Henry Crabb Robinson, and Mrs. Oliphant. Scott by 1826 had read it "for the third time at least"; for the nineteen-year-old Anthony Trollope it was "the best novel in the English Language"; George Henry Lewes said in 1847 that he "would rather have written [it] . . . than any of the Waverley Novels," and a dozen years later, claiming to have reread all the novels four times (on at least some of those occasions in the company of George Eliot), found in it "the best story, and the greatest variety of character . . . the interest is unflagging." The chorus of acclamation was not unanimous, of course, but even the depreciators tended to make *Pride and Prejudice* the favorite target for their strictures and thus to acknowledge its special standing. Charlotte Brontë's failure to see very much in it is notorious, and it was this novel (with *Sense and Sensibility*) which made Mark Twain "feel like a barkeeper entering the Kingdom of Heaven."[3] While some of the other five novels won their supporters, it was not in such numbers as this one. *Mansfield Park*, ignored by the reviewers, was enjoyed by Maria Edgeworth; Whateley found in it "some of Miss Austen's best moral lessons, as well as her most humorous descriptions"; and later in the century Julia Kavanagh recorded that it was "in the opinion of many, [her] most perfect novel," though another lady reader, Mrs. Oliphant, considered it "the least striking of the whole series . . . dull and lengthy as a whole, and not agreeable." *Emma* was voted best on several occasions—by Pollock, for example, in 1860 and by E. V. Lucas just after the turn of the century—but its nineteenth-century reception offered no foreshadowing of its present status. The other three novels were never serious contenders for the palm, though the *British Critic* in 1818 put on record the surprising opinion that *Northanger Abbey* was "one of the very best of Miss Austen's productions." The qualities of *Persuasion* went generally unrecognized; in the estimation of Lewes, indeed, it was the weakest of the set, and Whateley's view that it was the finest was strikingly unconventional.

For the nineteenth century, then, *Pride and Prejudice* was widely recognized as *the* Austen novel; and when Victorian reviewers felt moved to recite a muster roll of classic English novels, it is, in the company of *Tom Jones* and so forth, practically always the one chosen to represent Jane Austen. One is impelled to wonder why there should have been this consensus, what qualities in the novel commended it so vigorously and outstandingly to nineteenth-century readers, and why so ready an assent to its supremacy would almost certainly not be forthcoming from a majority of academic readers today. And, if *Pride and Prejudice* is now often rivalled or ousted by other contenders, it ought to be possible to say what we are able to find in them which our predecessors were unable to find, or perhaps not even interested in looking for.

It needs to be said first, however, that in a very real sense critical prejudice has not deprived the nineteenth century's favorite Austen novel from pride of place; for it continues to hold the lead, if one is to judge by the simple measuring device of the number of editions and reprints currently available. Both the British and the American editions of *Books in Print* show it well ahead in the field; *Emma* takes second place; and surprisingly *Sense and Sensibility* beats *Mansfield Park* by a short head on both sides of the Atlantic. Now all this may reflect little more than the conservative tradition of a pedagogical rearguard, since many of the copies sold no doubt find a haven in the classroom and the college library. But the preferences of the common reader may also help to determine this statistically dictated order of merit; and it is surely revealing that *Pride and Prejudice* is the only novel of the six to have reached large audiences through the medium of the cinema (though the omnivorous medium of television has more recently committed assault in quest of material upon some of the others).

It is worth remembering, then, that the attentions of critics, scholars, thesis-writers, and the academic establishment in general provide only one means of estimating literary honors and that readers at large may return different answers to the same questions. When all the ironies and ambiguities that the modern student has been trained to detect and evaluate have been given due weight, the enduring appeal of *Pride and Prejudice* is the strong but simple one of two abidingly popular forms. It is both a love story and a comedy and stands among the highest achievements in both directions. As a love story, its plot-lines lead inevitably to the altar; yet one might go further and suggest that its originality and interest are even higher than some of its admirers would claim; for it contrives to lend unfamiliar depth to its fairly conventional situations and to explore the failure of the course of true love to run smooth with a psychological acuteness hitherto unknown in English fiction. (The only exception one might feel inclined to make is Richardson, who was, significantly, a major influence; but his extraordinary analytical power is brought to bear on a largely different range of temperaments and situations.) It is true that the novel's situations are, superficially considered, sufficiently hackneyed: one girl marries from motives of prudence, one through folly, one after overcoming obstacles erected by her lover's family, another after surmounting antipathy based on a misunderstanding of her lover's true nature. What holds together such a diverse set of characters as Charlotte and Lydia, Darcy and Wickham and Mr. Collins, is a concern, operating below the level of the shifts and figures of the narrative, with the nature of a good marriage. There is an authorial reference in the third volume to the "foundations of affection" (279), a phrase which seems to sum up a preoccupation in the novel at least as central as the more widely discussed issues embodied in the title; and the four marriages depicted—or five if we include, as I think we must, that of the Bennet parents—are case studies, of different degrees of complexity, in the factors making for success or failure in matrimony. Whereas most love stories imply a view of marriage as "the end of experience" (the phrase is Ursula's in *Women in Love*), *Pride and Prejudice* shows it as a dynamic state of life directly determined by the soundness of the alliance that has been formed and the motives and principles that have produced it. If *Pride and Prejudice* is a love story (and generations of readers have taken it primarily as such), it is so in the perhaps unusual sense of seeing courtship as a phase and not as an end in itself.

That comedy is not the inevitable mode for the presentation of such a theme was to be demonstrated later in the century by *Middlemarch* and *The Portrait of a Lady*. But, as well as being a very serious book, *Pride and Prejudice* is also a very funny one, the wittiest as well as the most dramatic of the novels—dramatic, that is, in the manner of stage comedy, of which we are irresistibly reminded in scene after scene, from the domestic conversation of the opening chapter to the magnificent repartees of Elizabeth's final encounter with Lady Catherine de Bourgh. Local delight in phrase and episode, combined with a theme both traditionally popular and unconventionally profound in its handling: this formula would appear to be sufficient to guarantee the novel's popularity, then and now. We must add that the heroine not only seems to enjoy the author's special sympathy and approval, but that the reader is likely to have fewer reservations concerning her than are prompted by other Austen heroines. Looking back to Rosalind and Portia and forward to Trollope's Lily Dale, George Eliot's Gwendolen Harleth, and James's Isabel Archer, Elizabeth Bennet stands in her own great tradition of liberated women, their intelligence and articulateness enabling them not merely to survive in a man's world—that world in which, as Anne Elliot later points out, men have written all the books and thus imposed their own version of reality—but to show up their males as relatively dull and conventional.

For the common reader of the late twentieth century, these qualities have lost none of their luster; but as early as 1870 we find the more rigorous critic distinguishing between the earlier "trilogy" of *Pride and Prejudice*, *Sense and Sensibility* and *Northanger Abbey*, and the later, consisting of *Mansfield Park*, *Emma* and *Persuasion*. For Richard Simpson (perhaps under the influence of his studies of Shakespeare's dramatic development), the latter group is "a kind of reproduction of the former, in the light of a maturer knowledge": he finds Jane Austen covering "the same ground, trying other ways of producing the same effects" (Southam, pp. 253, 257). While recognizing the family likeness between the novels, he detects in the canon two distinct levels of maturity, with *Pride and Prejudice* located firmly in the earlier phase. More recent critics have often concurred in seeing it as the climax of a phase of development in which Jane Austen was still deeply indebted to eighteenth-century literary and moral traditions. Avrom Fleishman, for instance, writes that "whereas Elizabeth Bennet ends a century, Fanny Price begins one."[4] Although, in common with many a later nineteenth-century heroine, she is certainly engaged in a voyage of self-discovery, Elizabeth may strike the student nurtured on post-Austenite fiction as too serenely confident and good-humored for his taste: she is not Sue Bridehead, nor was meant to be. Fanny Price, on the other hand, has *Angst* enough and to spare. As we have seen, most of Jane Austen's immediate circle of readers gave *Mansfield Park* second place to *Pride and Prejudice;* one suspects, however, that most academic courses on the novel in our time (for what such an index of esteem or value is worth), as well as many critics and readers, would reverse this judgment.

Admittedly the reaction of those first readers is one we can understand, even if we do not share it. A novel which speaks out against vivacity, wit, and "style" in social relationships–Edmund's reference to the "too lively mind" (421) of Mary Crawford is endorsed by the authorial voice, which can also speak in passing of "a family of lively agreeable manners, and probably of morals and discretion to suit" (450)–seems to have the effect of devaluing the very qualities for which Elizabeth Bennet is admired and invites admiration. And too much seems to me to have been made of the novel's humor: Lady Bertram, so often invoked as a comic figure, is treated with real savagery at times, notably in volume 3, chapter 13; and if Mrs. Norris, self-importantly fussing over green baize and pheasants' eggs, is sometimes a figure of absurdity, the moral verdict on her is consistently merciless, from her fraudulent part in bringing Fanny to Mansfield Park to her final relegation to a kind of purgatory. The kinds of interest which *Pride and Prejudice* offers cannot be readily discovered in the later novel: the element of comedy is muted; the love story, though important, runs below surface for much of the time, rather than erupting in dramatic confrontation; and the heroine, though estimable, is less obviously appealing–not so much a Rosalind as a female Nathaniel (for Edmund she is "the heart which knew no guile" [455]). Yet Fanny perhaps deserves a better and more sympathetic press than she has generally received; indeed, such diatribes as Reginald Farrer's ("female prig-pharisee . . . repulsive in her cast-iron self-righteousness"[5]) make one wonder if one has been reading the same novel. Some of Fanny's critics seem to have been surprised that she should not have had the temperament of an Emma Woodhouse, when her situation in fact more closely resembles that of Oliver Twist. Her intense shyness, given her circumstances and the figures who populate her world, is surely less surprising than its opposite would be; and her quiet, self-effacing nature in the event gives her a more reliable point of view and enables her to judge more clearly than those who enter more fully into the world's pleasures. Thomas Hardy once wrote in his diary: "If

I were a painter, I would paint a picture of a room as viewed by a mouse from a chink under the skirting."[6] Fanny may be a mouse, but from her unobtrusive vantage point she *sees.* Her observation of the Portsmouth ménage, "the walls marked by her father's head," and "the milk [on the tea table] a mixture of motes floating in thin blue" (439), produces the most brilliant passage of naturalistic description in Jane Austen's novels. It is surely unfair, and inaccurate, to call Fanny a prig: serious, even humorless, she is, but designedly so in a novel which is concerned to demonstrate the perils of levity, one which its author herself characterized as involving "a complete change of subject" from that of *Pride and Prejudice,* and for which she claimed the overriding quality not of "wit" but of "good sense" (*Letters,* 298, 443). Whatever we may think of Fanny Price, we cannot put her down to miscalculation on her creator's part.

The absence of the qualities which have made *Pride and Prejudice* an enduring popular success has withheld this kind of acclaim from *Mansfield Park;* at the same time, the fascination of what's difficult in the problems raised by its seriousness, and especially by the paradox of its deliberate and puzzling plea for stasis and dullness, have granted it a critical and academic reputation of the highest order—not surprisingly perhaps in a generation which has effected similar revaluations in respect of other novelists. The same readers who prefer *Little Dorrit* to *Pickwick Papers* are likely to give *Mansfield Park* preference over *Pride and Prejudice,* whereas the Victorian idolater of *Pickwick* who complained that Dickens did not continue writing in the same vein may well have been the same reader who set *Pride and Prejudice* above the rest of Jane Austen's work. Such judgments perhaps tell us less about the novels in question than about the limitations of novel-readers, including the professional reviewers, for most of whom, at least until the later nineteenth-century, Scott and the eighteenth-century novelists provided a rarely questioned yardstick. (Scott, who had high praise for *Emma,* ignored *Mansfield Park* completely, much to Jane Austen's chagrin: see *Letters*, 453.) As succeeding generations, thanks to James and others, learned not only to read a new kind of novel but to read older novels in a new way, *Mansfield Park* began to win belated recognition. If we read it as a nineteenth-century reader might have done, we can understand the recorded reactions which so often seem curiously wide of the mark—Whateley, for instance, whose favorite it was, finding in it some admirable "moral lessons" but being apparently blind to the much more impressive moral and psychological drama of Fanny's predicament. But we see it as something quite different, and considerably richer, if we read it as if it had been written not by a contemporary of Sir Walter Scott but by, say, the George Eliot of *Middlemarch* and *Daniel Deronda*. Such a reading will give due weight to elements in the novel—the complexity of Mary Crawford's character, the significance of the country house, the symbolism of the scene in the "wilderness" at Sotherton, and others—of which the nineteenth-century reader may have been hardly aware.

For F. R. Leavis, Jane Austen's status as "the inaugurator of the great tradition of the English novel" rests upon two major characteristics of her work: her "intense moral preoccupation" and her concern with form.[7] Neither, one suspects, would have ranked very high on the list of fictional desiderata for most nineteenth-century readers. "Wholesomeness," as reviewers tended to call it, was a requisite of fiction intended for family consumption, but it was generally understood to consist in the *absence* of certain elements, while the interpolated sermons, long and short, found in many Victorian novels scarcely constitute "moral preoccupation," and "form" was rarely heard of in relation to the novel. As late as 1859, as intelligent and enthusiastic a critic as Lewes could find only the most simplistic terms (already quoted) in which to praise *Pride and Prejudice*. Small wonder that the moral debate of *Mansfield Park* went generally unheeded and that it was left to our own century to discover the formal and technical excellence of *Emma.* It seems to have been R. W. Chapman who in 1922 first drew attention to the Jamesian qualities of the latter novel—a cue promptly taken up by Virginia Woolf and, in different terms, by Kipling in his story "The Janeites."[8]

Why should the nineteenth century have failed to respond so keenly to the merits of *Emma* as its post-Jamesian and presentday readers? Jane Austen perhaps anticipated this question in her celebrated diagnosis of her heroine's likely lack of appeal (one whom "no one but myself will much like"). The different degrees of acceptability of Elizabeth Bennet and Emma Woodhouse suggest that the earlier readers demanded a heroine on whom they could bestow moral approval and emotional sympathy without reservations. As a result, the modern reader often finds himself differing from earlier estimates of certain characters as well as from what appear to have been the author's own attitudes: we are likely to find Estella more interesting than Little Nell and perhaps even to prefer Rosamund Vincy as a psychological portrait to Dorothea Brooke. Another cause for Victorian dissatisfaction with *Emma* was the lack of action: an age which had come to take for granted in its fiction a well-made plot with moving accidents in every other chapter must have felt somewhat cheated by a novel in which the events rarely rise above the narrative excitement of a picnic, a strawberry party, or a morning call. Henry Crabb Robinson, who had been delighted by *Pride and Prejudice*, found *Emma* "not interesting," and John Henry Newman was no doubt typical of many others in complaining that the action was confined to "trifles." A *Westminster Review* article of 1853 recognizes Jane Austen as "a true artist" but makes a similar complaint that her scenes confine themselves too exclusively to "the littlenesses and trivialities of life." (If that article is, as Professor Haight suggests, by George Eliot, it is noteworthy that it should have appeared in the same decade as *Adam Bede*, with its paraphernalia of seduction, child-murder, death-sentence, and last-minute reprieve: weighing the artistic success of *Emma* against that novel provides both a sufficient answer to the *Westminster*'s criticisms and an illuminating contrast between the art of Jane Austen and the state of the novel in the fifties.) There were, of course, nineteenth-century defenders of *Emma*, of whom the earliest and most notable was Scott. Had his *Quarterly* article been more carefully studied by Victorian novelists and reviewers, his own novels might have been less often taken as models, and criticism of the novel in the next two or three generations might have gained considerably. By and large, however, *Emma* seems to have enjoyed markedly less esteem than *Pride and Prejudice* for at least a hundred years, though subsequent critics have gone far towards reversing this judgment.

If we have learned anything from the Jamesian and the Woolfian novel, it is that lack of dramatic action and apparent triviality of plot-material constitute no grounds for complaint. Indeed, James's claim that "the high attributes of a subject" can be found in "the mere slim shade of an intelligent but presumptuous girl" might almost have been written as a defense of the method of *Emma*. It is not merely that the Jamesian novel owes something to *Emma:* without going all the way with Borges, who in an interesting essay on Kafka argues that a writer creates his own precursors, we may agree that we needed James in order to show us how properly to read Austen. It will not do, however, to stress the formal and technical qualities of the book—striking though these are in their skill and originality—to the total neglect of the basis of its popular appeal. For, if one ceases to worry about the heroine's shortcomings, it can be seen as a book of marvellously inventive comedy: the often bitter censoriousness of *Mansfield Park* has disappeared, and Mr. Woodhouse and Miss Bates and even the Eltons, who would surely have been portrayed in darker tones in the earlier novel, are figures who, since nearly all the comedy derives from their speech, have a comic and dramatic power which it is not extravagant to compare (as Lewes, to his undying credit, did) to Shakespeare.

Since, though one would not wish to be without them, neither

Northanger Abbey nor *Sense and Sensibility* has ever been a serious contender for supremacy, what of *Persuasion*, the most consistently undervalued of the six novels? Anne Elliot is almost wholly selfeffacing: until the magnificent penultimate chapter, perhaps no heroine in fiction speaks so little. It is as if, after showing her mastery of dialogue, Jane Austen were setting herself an entirely different problem: to render what she calls in the cancelled chapter the "silent but . . . very powerful dialogue" of feelings of which social custom and personal inhibitions alike forbid the expression. In this least dramatic of the novels, the hero and heroine hardly speak to each other in the first volume—which is not to say that they do not communicate, for the intensity of their inner lives is manifested by look, facial expression, and action. Since the viewpoint is Anne's, her thoughts and feelings can be made fully available to the reader throughout, even when they misinterpret and mislead, as in her mistake over Lady Russell's scrutiny of the "window-curtains" (179); but Wentworth, who is seen almost wholly from the outside, is reduced to expressive behavior, of which some examples follow:

> Captain Wentworth left his seat, and walked to the fireplace; probably for the sake of walking away from it soon afterwards, and taking a station, with less bare-faced design, by Anne. (225)

> Captain Wentworth looked round at her instantly in a way which shewed his noticing of it. He gave her a momentary glance,—a glance of brightness, which seemed to say . . . (104)

> He turned round the next instant to give a look—one quick, conscious look at her. (231)

> Anne caught his eye, saw his cheeks glow, and his mouth form itself into a momentary expression of contempt, and turned away. (227)

> She received no other answer, than an artificial, assenting

> smile, followed by a contemptuous glance, as he turned away, which Anne perfectly knew the meaning of. (86)

That *probably* in my first example suggests the limited nature of the reader's access to Wentworth's consciousness, while the final clause of the last quotation identifies Anne as a uniquely qualified interpreter of signs. These moments are often vividly rendered, though on occasion (as in the last two examples) Jane Austen slips into staginess. Such local blemishes are of minor importance, however, and, given the nature of her method, are perhaps inevitable. Whereas Elizabeth and Darcy, and later Emma and Mr. Knightley, work out their changing relationships through conversation, Anne and Wentworth *watch* each other. The characteristic technique has shifted from dramatic dialogue to inner speech; and, as I have tried to show elsewhere,[9] *Persuasion* is, in its free blending of narrative, dialogue, and a kind of interior monologue, an extraordinary technical achievement which was in its originality and artistry to have no parallel for many decades. Anne has no gift, or indeed opportunity, as a debater: her forte is "quiet observation" (34) and strong but undisclosed feelings. Other heroines participate; she overhears (in chapter 10 through a hedge, in chapter 12 through an open door, and in the cancelled chapter through a closed one). Even Wentworth's declaration of love dispenses with the spoken word: like the most obsessive of epistolary characters, he writes a letter to Anne while in the same room with her and delivers it "with eyes of glowing entreaty fixed on her for a moment" (236), but without uttering a syllable. Small wonder that, when their love is acknowledged and their vow of silence can be broken, "All the little variations of the last week were gone through; and of yesterday and to-day there could scarcely be an end" (241)—though, significantly, much of this scene of mutual enlightenment is conducted through narrative rather than direct speech.

What has been said perhaps accounts sufficiently for the relative neglect of *Persuasion:* readers who cast Jane Austen as a writer of "brilliant" dialogue, witty, epigrammatic and satirical, and as the creator of "sparkling" heroines—notions not so much wrongheaded, of course, as incomplete—must often have been puzzled and disappointed by this final novel, a deeply emotional book which ranges from introspective melancholy to "private rapture" (240). It falls short of structural perfection: Mrs. Smith and Captain Benwick, for instance, are somewhat awkward and embarrassing pieces of machinery; but in control of emotional tone and narrative voice it ought to stand very high in the Austen canon and much higher in nineteenth-century fiction than has usually been admitted. Ultimately, though, to suggest that *Persuasion* and in some respects *Mansfield Park* have received less than their due is not to lessen one's sense of the achievements of *Pride and Prejudice* and *Emma*, though the qualities most persistently associated with Jane Austen derive more obviously from the latter than from the former pair of novels. The final effect of such a readjustment should be to increase our awareness of the range of her art—she is much less of a small neat classic than the general estimates of either century have held—and of the differences between the novels, surely so much more striking and interesting than the similarities.

NOTES

1. This and most of the other nineteenth-century critical assessments cited are conveniently collected by B. C. Southam in *Jane Austen: The Critical Heritage* (London: Routledge and Kegan Paul, 1968). The passage by Pollock appears on p. 168.

2. Reprinted in Southam, pp. 48-57.

3. See Joseph Cady and Ian Watt, "Jane Austen's Critics," *Critical Quarterly*, 5 (1963), 54.

4. *A Reading of "Mansfield Park"* (Minneapolis: University of Minnesota Press, 1967), p. 73.

5. "Jane Austen, *ob.* July 18, 1817," *Quarterly Review*, 228 (July 1917), p. 22.

6. F. E. Hardy, *The Life of Thomas Hardy, 1840-1928* (London: Macmillan, 1962), p. 235.

7. *The Great Tradition* (London: Chatto and Windus, 1948), p. 7.

8. Chapman's suggestion (in the *Times Literary Supplement*) was quickly followed by Virginia Woolf's remark (in the *Nation*, 15 December 1923) that Jane Austen "would (if she had lived) have been the forerunner of Henry James and Proust," and by Kipling's story (first published 1924). See Chapman, *Jane Austen: a Critical Bibliography*, 2nd ed. (London: Oxford University Press, 1955), p. 44.

9. "Categories of Speech in *Persuasion*," *Modern Language Review*, 64 (1969), 734-741.

ROBERT ALAN DONOVAN

THE MIND OF JANE AUSTEN

The appearance in 1932 of the Clarendon Press edition of Jane Austen's letters profoundly disillusioned some of the more fastidious admirers of her novels. While praising Chapman's meticulous editing, both Harold Nicolson and E. M. Forster professed themselves disenchanted with the triviality of the letters and the vulgarity of the mind which produced them.[1] Nicolson compares Jane Austen's mind to "a very small, sharp pair of scissors, attached by a pink ribbon to a very neat and maidenly work basket," but what really offends him is her "parlour refinement," her "appalling gentility of style." Forster hears the voice of Lydia Bennet in the early letters: "balls, officers, giggling, dresses, officers, balls,"[2] and the stately and pompous accents of Sir Thomas Bertram in the later ones, catching no echo of any of the more lively and attractive characters in the novels.

Both Nicolson and Forster find it difficult to understand how the same mind could have produced these letters and the novels, and both offer hypotheses to account for the disparity. Nicolson attributes the flatness of the letters to the closeness of the intimacy betwen Jane and Cassandra (to whom most of the letters are addressed) and to the dullness of Cassandra. Forster chooses to distinguish absolutely betwen the letter-writer, "Miss Austen," and the novelist, "Jane Austen," on the grounds that the narrowness of Miss Austen's world failed to offer the intellectual stimulation that might have animated her pen: "She has not enough subject-matter on which to exercise her powers. Her character and sex as well as her environment removed her from public affairs, and she was too sincere and spontaneous to affect any interest which she does not feel." Only occasionally does the dull routine of her life startle her into the acuteness and clarity of perception which characterizes the novels at their best.

Neither Nicolson nor Forster can be said to misrepresent the letters, which *do* deal wearisomely with details of dress and household management and with personalities too well known to the correspondents for any effort to make them interesting to a third person. What is perhaps more questionable in these critical responses is the implicit assumption that great novelistic art must be nourished by a spacious intellectual and social milieu, that the distinguishing attribute of such art is its urbanity. Neither critic, presumably, finds it surprising to discover that the maiden daughter of a country parson could write such letters; both find it all but incredible that she could also write *Pride and Prejudice* or *Persuasion.* The attitude implied by Nicolson's scissors simile, particularly in the gratuitous elaboration of the pink ribbon, is not simply what is now called sexism; for it refers not only to sex, but also to class, situation, and intellectual style. Jane Austen's letters come as a trouble to Nicolson's and Forster's joy in the novels, and it is difficult to avoid the suspicion that they were disturbed especially by the discovery that she was not one of themselves.

Such snobbishness (for it deserves no softer name) reveals itself most clearly in comments about language or style. Nicolson assails her "appalling gentility," and Forster her "ill-breeding and . . . sententiousness," but the comments tell us more about their authors' tastes and values than about Jane Austen's artistry or lack of it. On special occasions—the death of a family member or of a public figure—Jane Austen writes in the conventional language of piety. One cannot very well impugn her sincerity on these occasions, but Forster does fault her for what he obviously feels is a defect of taste, a want of urbanity, in employing a vocabulary and a rhetoric characteristic of, if not peculiar to, the Anglican establishment before the Oxford movement. The style is alien and repugnant to Forster, but he is mistaken, surely, in inferring from it any fundamental defect of thought or feeling. Those who on occasion use language they have been conditioned to think appropriate to the occasion are not necessarily either hypocritical or weak-minded, and Forster concedes as much when he writes of Henry Thornton that "his exhortations were sincere, like everything else he wrote or did . . . but the words he used—like many of the words then used—will not travel."[3] His judgment of the man's character and intellect rises superior to his distaste for the jargon of Clapham.

Nicolson's and Forster's reactions to the letters were expressed in articles written for weekly reviews in 1932. At this distance they are scarcely important enough to warrant refutation, but they suggest a useful paradigm of critical attitudes toward Jane Austen's mind and art which are no less persistent because they are at least as often implied as stated. I think it is time to call into question some of these attitudes, among which should be mentioned the views that Jane Austen is essentially an ironist intent on discrediting the values of the society she portrays, that she cannot represent what she has never experienced, that (consequently) the perfection of her art derives from the deliberate limitation of her *mundus representandi*, that she is deficient in the portrayal of feelings, and that her ability to transmute the materials of ordinary experience into art depends on a quality of mind which may be variously defined, but which is conspicuously absent from the letters.

I have neither the temerity nor the desire to challenge, piecemeal or entire, the body of criticism in which the foregoing attitudes may be read. I suggest only that such criticism has frequently operated within a tacit framework of assumptions about

Jane Austen's mind, assumptions which at once concede too much and too little—too much if they make the operative faculty of her art a formidable but mainly abstract power of analysis or synthesis, too little if they see her art as mysteriously achieved in the face of an imaginative impotence which keeps her from delineating what she has never seen or felt. In short, I should like to explore a hypothesis contrary to Forster's, that the recorder of daily trivia and the creative artist, the letter-writer and the novelist, Miss Austen and Jane Austen, are one and the same.

The notion that Jane Austen's art obeys an impulse which is primarily subversive arises, no doubt, from the observation that her ironic thorns tend to be found in the midst of blander, more innocuous growths, that her irony redoubles its effect by flashing out of passages of description or commentary which are complacent, or even laudatory. To give only one of many examples, Henry Tilney, in describing the generally beneficent forces in modern society tending to regulate human conduct, includes the observation that "every man is surrounded by a neighbourhood of voluntary spies" (*NA*, 197-198).[4] It may be doubted, however, that such ironic sallies have the power of converting everything they touch into their own nature and substance. It seems far more likely that they are the spontaneous eruptions of malice, engendered as much by impatience with pomposity or decorum as by a deeply considered or matured social attitude. Jane Austen was capable of writing to her sister in a strain quite revolting to many readers: "Mrs. Hall, of Sherborne, was brought to bed yesterday of a dead child, some weeks before she expected, owing to a fright. I suppose she happened unawares to look at her husband" (24). But she is simply obeying the same impish prompting which leads Emma to make fun of Miss Bates at Box Hill—the sudden and overwhelming impulse to treat irreverently what we have been taught to regard with respect and solemnity. The difference, of course, is that Emma's witticism is uttered publicly so that it wounds its victim at the same time that it assaults decorum and thus merits Mr. Knightley's rebuke (*E*, 370-376). Anne Elliot, much more restrained than Emma, nevertheless understands the impulse when she is confronted by the spectacle of the portly Mrs. Musgrove mourning her son: "A large bulky figure has as good a right to be in deep affliction as the most graceful set of limbs in the world. But, fair or not fair, there are unbecoming conjunctions, which reason will patronize in vain,—which taste cannot tolerate,—which ridicule will seize" (*P*, 68). That human beings take pleasure in malice is shocking only to postromantic idealism; Jane Austen shared with her older contemporary, Jeremy Bentham, the recognition that it is as human to take delight in malevolence as in benevolence, and Dr. Johnson himself might have applauded her attempts to shake her mind free of cant.

Jane Austen's irony is pervasive, but it is not always irreverent, nor is it necessarily inconsistent with other narrative modes, including those which are morally committed. Irony is commonly destructive in that it serves to deflate pretense. Such irony takes no moral position itself, but merely reveals the disparity between our professed motives and our real ones. There is also, however, another kind of irony, which may as in Swift be yoked to moralizing or didactic purposes. It differs from destructive irony by being morally committed, by revealing the disparity between an approved ideal of conduct and whatever violates that ideal. When we read in *Mansfield Park* that "the approach of September brought tidings of Mr. Bertram first in a letter to the gamekeeper, and then in a letter to Edmund" (114), we are conscious of an incongruity between Tom's self-indulgence and the respect he owes to his family.[5] The irony is in no way weakened by the fact that the narrator has clearly implied her own moral vantage point.

Such morally focused irony is more consistent with Jane Austen's characteristic narrative stance than the stray shafts of malice that critics have so often seized upon. Struck by the hard brilliance of her irony, readers are not perhaps so inclined to notice the persistent moralizing bent of her prose. This bent reveals itself in several ways, most obviously no doubt in the moral valuations passed by the narrator (whether ironically or not), but more significantly, and in a manner more uniquely characteristic of Jane Austen's style, in her fondness for what used to be called sentences—generalized reflections about life, often aphoristic in form, nearly always moral in tendency. Sentences, in this old-fashioned sense, are a principal source of comedy in *Pride and Prejudice*, which opens with a superb ironic example of the form—"It is a truth universally acknowledged, that a single man in possession of a good fortune, must be in want of a wife" (2)—and then proceeds to parade before the reader a succession of absurdly pompous pronouncements by Mary Bennet (20), Charlotte Lucas (21), and Mr. Collins (101, et passim). But sententious utterance is a habit even with many characters who are clearly meant to be taken seriously: both Marianne and Elinor Dashwood, for example, as well as Edmund Bertram, Henry Tilney, and Mr. Knightley. It is important, however, to see the sententious style as expressing a characteristic motion of Jane Austen's own mind, not just as a device of characterization; accordingly, none of the examples which follow is taken from passages of dialogue. At one extreme are those finely honed and pointed examples which one would seek in vain in the letters—generalized reflections which achieve the conciseness and the pointedness of aphorisms:

> When people are determined on a mode of conduct which they know to be wrong, they feel injured by the expectation of any thing better from them (*SS*, 248-249).
>
> She found, what has been sometimes found before, that an event to which she had looked forward with impatient desire, did not, in taking place, bring all the satisfaction she had promised herself (*PP*, 237).
>
> A sanguine temper, though for ever expecting more good than occurs, does not always pay for its hopes by any proportionate depression (*E*, 144).

> To come with a well-informed mind, is to come with an inability of administering to the vanity of others (*NA*, 110).

> The public . . . is rather apt to be unreasonably discontented when a woman *does* marry again, than when she does *not* (*P*, 5).

> How quick come the reasons for approving what we like! (*P*, 15).

Still more numerous, and thus more characteristic, are those moralizing passages which, without any attempt to achieve aphoristic concision or point, content themselves with the expression of traditional or even commonplace wisdom as it relates to characters or situations:

> [Elinor's] thoughts were silently fixed on the irreparable injury which too early an independence and its consequent habits of idleness, dissipation, and luxury, had made in the mind, the character, the happiness, of a man who, to every advantage of person and talents, united a disposition naturally open and honest (*SS*, 331).

> If gratitude and esteem are good foundations of affection, Elizabeth's change of sentiment will be neither improbable nor faulty (*PP*, 279).

> How little of permanent happiness could belong to a couple who were only brought together because their passions were stronger than their virtue (*PP*, 312).

> How wretched, and how unpardonable, how hopeless and wicked it [is], to marry without affection (*MP*, 324).

> There was something honourable and valuable in the strong domestic habits, the all-sufficiency of home to himself, whence resulted her brother's disposition to look down on the common rate of social intercourse, and those to whom it was important (*E*, 97).

> A submissive spirit might be patient, a strong understanding would supply resolution, but here was something more:

> here was that elasticity of mind, that disposition to be comforted, that power of turning readily from evil to good, and of finding employment which carried her out of herself, which was from Nature alone (*P*, 154).[6]

I do not think we have given sufficient weight to this side of Jane Austen's mind and art. Her lively sense of the ridiculous, the wit which can accomplish such dazzling changes of pace or tone, have their undoubted charm, but they should not be permitted to obscure the fundamental gravity of her attitude toward life. All her sprightliness, as well as all her apparent preoccupation with the minutiae of daily life, are merely the superficial motions of a mind which is anchored in conventional pieties and the moral imperatives which derive from them. Although she writes, in her letters and in her novels, of common life, it would be a mistake to assume that her principal literary antecedents include such writers as Cowper and Wordsworth (Forster, rejecting Chapman's claim that she has all of Cowper's sense of charm in little things, sees her as a kind of failed Cowper). The moral sententiousness which both Forster and Nicolson complain of in the letters is, as I have tried to show, still more pervasive in the novels. Because she looks at actions and characters in relation to moral principles which can be universalized, she is fundamentally a moralist, in the same sense that Pope and Johnson are.

Even more persistent than the view of Jane Austen as primarily a satirist is the notion that her stature as a novelist is diminished by the narrowness of her range. She herself has been at least partly to blame for the widespread belief that she cannot render anything beyond the range of her immediate observation,[7] because of the advice she gave to her niece, Anna Austen, who was (in the summer of 1814) at work on a novel: "We think you had better not leave England. Let the Portmans go to Ireland, but as you know nothing of the Manners there, you had better not go with them. You will be in danger of giving false representations. Stick to Bath & the Foresters. There you will be quite at home"

(*Letters*, 395). But the caution expressed here has a limited applicability to the exercise of the novelist's imagination. Verisimilitude in detail, which Jane Austen highly prized in her own work, is clearly the value her advice to Anna was intended to secure, and there is evidence that Jane Austen occasionally made a show of such verisimilitude for its own sake. Her indulgence in the technical jargon of seamanship, for example, in *Mansfield Park* (380) and again in *Persuasion* (108) does not have the excuse of necessity; like Charlotte Brontë's French, it is put in merely to show that she can speak the language. A far more important kind of truth than that which can be ensured by an intimate knowledge of the "manners" of a particular locale is the rightness with which the novelist renders the felt quality of the life he describes. It demands a fidelity not only to the facts of experience, but also to the configuration or meaning of those facts which his unique imaginative vision necessarily supplies. This kind of truth owes less to the novelist's powers and range of observation than to his insight and imagination.

In a well-known anecdote Henry James illustrates the creative process by which one novelist succeeded in rendering a particular pattern and way of life with admirable realism. Her experience of that way of life was acquired by a momentary glimpse through an open doorway as she ascended the stair. James refers this miracle to "the faculty which when you give it an inch takes an ell, and which for the artist is a much greater source of strength than any accident of residence or of place in the social scale. The power to guess the unseen from the seen, to trace the implication of things, to judge the whole piece by the pattern, the condition of feeling life in general so completely that you are well on your way to knowing any particular corner of it—this cluster of gifts may almost be said to constitute experience."[8] Insofar as Jane Austen's novels constitute a detailed record of daily life, they remain rigorously within the limits of her observation. Insofar as they attempt to be more and to provide imaginative glimpses of human possibility within a specific social milieu, observation gives way to experience, defined not as an "accident of residence" but as a "cluster of gifts." Observation can give us such quasi-Dickensian portraits as those of Mr. Collins or Mrs. Norris, but it requires imaginative insight, "experience," in James's sense, to reveal to us the shattering collapse of Emma Woodhouse's illusions about herself, or to let us see into the exulting heart of Anne Elliot. In the most literal sense Jane Austen accepted her own advice to remain within the limits of firsthand observation, but the special quality or power of her art derives from the fact that the world of her observation is only the surface aspect of a much larger imagined world.

Jane Austen's more sympathetic critics make a virtue of what her detractors think of as her narrowness and indeed see the perfection of her art in its deliberate, self-imposed limitations. It must be admitted that the represented world of her novels, as has often been pointed out, is curiously confined. References to contemporary public events are infrequent and indirect. If it were not for the militia billeted in Meryton or Frederick Wentworth's prize money we might not suspect that England was at war during most of the period represented in the novels. More curious still, at least for us, in an age in which fiction has become an arm of sociology, is the absence of any attempt to render the red or violet ends of the English social spectrum. We are shown very little of the authentic aristocracy and still less of the lower orders of society. Although virtually all the characters of these novels move through rooms thickly tenanted with servants, the servants remain shadowy figures. We do not see their faces, or hear their voices, or (with few exceptions) know their names.

One reason for such a drastic restriction of the represented world is suggested by Jane Austen's own fanciful metaphor of painting "two inches of ivory" with a fine brush. The art of the miniaturist is above all an art of selection and isolation, aiming at charm and delicacy rather than richness or variety or strength; and many readers, accepting the implied valuation, have turned away from Jane Austen in the quite mistaken belief that no strong wine can be pressed from such carefully pruned vines. They forget that all the Romanée Conti in the world is grown on four-and-a-half acres of the Côte d'Or. The fact is that Jane Austen's is not a miniaturist's art at all, however small the surface on which she chooses to work. Reduction of scale must not be confused with concentration of effect, and it is concentration of effect which gives strength and vigor to these novels. The ivory cameo is as misleading a metaphor as Nicholson's "neat and maidenly work basket."

A minor but suggestive indication of the extent to which Jane Austen's novels are the product of an imaginative effort far exceeding what might be inferred from their relatively tranquil surface is to be found in the Austen family tradition, recorded by her nephew, that her characters had a life beyond the novels in which they occur:

> She would, if asked, tell us many little particulars about the subsequent career of some of her people. In this traditionary way we learned that Miss Steele never succeeded in catching the Doctor; that Kitty Bennet was satisfactorily married to a clergyman near Pemberley, while Mary obtained nothing higher than one of her uncle Philip's clerks, and was content to be considered a star in the society of Meriton; that the "considerable sum" given by Mrs. Norris to William Price was one pound; that Mr. Woodhouse survived his daughter's marriage, and kept her and Mr. Knightley from settling at Donwell, about two years; and that the letters placed by Frank Churchill before Jane Fairfax, which she swept away unread, contained the word "pardon."[9]

Virginia Woolf brings the practiced eye of a novelist to her reading of Jane Austen and helps us to understand the sources of that "peculiar intensity which she alone can impart." Her analysis of the opening pages of *The Watsons* transforms the effect from a conjuring trick into a product of the writer's least dramatic but most powerful weapon—excision. Because Jane Austen has imagined much more than she tells us, or needs to tell us, her pages are charged with a unique energy. "Jane Austen is thus a mistress of much deeper emotion than appears upon the surface. She stimulates us to supply what is not there."[10] It would be a mistake, however, to see Jane Austen's technique as essentially one of suggestion, for she succeeds less by encouraging the reader to invest her characters with his own spontaneous imaginings than by conveying the full rotundity of the figure in a faultlessly drawn line. The technique is fully under control, though it would be only fair to say that it is not always equally successful. Sometimes the characters get out of drawing, as when Lucy Steele makes a confidante of Elinor (*SS*, 128ff), or when Frederick Wentworth cries out for help after the accident on the Cobb (*P*, 110), but with those characters whom Jane Austen's imagination has fully seized and realized, even the minor touches are deft and unerring. When Elizabeth Bennet first catches sight of Pemberley and is struck by the reflection "that to be mistress of Pemberley might be something!" (*PP*, 245), a lesser writer might be tempted to try to persuade the reader that her feelings are disinterested, but Jane Austen's firm sense of her heroine's character can acknowledge no such need. She understands perfectly just how much of vanity and worldly regret enter into Elizabeth's feelings, but she also understands that these do not seriously undercut the emotion which is uppermost, an unaffected admiration for the vision of life which Pemberley embodies.

The impression of high intensity which Virginia Woolf has convincingly described, especially the intensity conveyed by passages of dialogue which contain very little overt expression of feeling, is more than a matter of our realizing that the characters are fully imagined, that they have secrets from us, passages in their past or future lives, that only accident will disclose to us. In such passages the energizing force is the result of an essentially dramatic irony. The characters, restrained by reticence or modesty, say less than is in their minds, their auditors seize different meanings from the one intended, and the reader becomes aware of subtle cross currents running beneath the surface of the dialogue.

The best example is to be found in the scene which effects the final rapprochement between Emma Woodhouse and Mr. Knightley (*E*, 424-433). Emma is walking in the shrubbery at Hartfield, trying to recover the tranquility which has been disturbed, first by the shattering disclosure that all her confident suppositions about others' feelings—and her own—have been mistaken, and secondly by the newly raised conjecture that Harriet Smith may have some ground for thinking Mr. Knightley in love with her, a possibility that is all the more agitating because Emma has just discovered the real nature of her own feelings toward Mr. Knightley. In this state of mind she is joined by Mr. Knightley, who has just come from London, and they fall into a conversation which, if one attends only to the words exchanged, is perfectly flat and commonplace, but which is stretched over a tense and highly charged encounter at the level of feeling. After the preliminary exchange of commonplace, even banal, greetings, during which each has an opportunity to sense the other's tension, Emma ventures on what appears to be nothing more than an item of local gossip:

> "You have some news to hear, now you are come back, that will rather surprise you."
>
> "Have I?" said he quietly, and looking at her; "of what nature?"
>
> "Oh! the best nature in the world—a wedding."
>
> After waiting a moment, as if to be sure she intended to to say no more, he replied,
>
> "If you mean Miss Fairfax and Frank Churchill, I have heard that already."
>
> "How is it possible?" cried Emma, turning her glowing cheeks towards him; for while she spoke, it occurred to her that he might have called at Mrs. Goddard's in his way.

> "I had a few lines on parish business from Mr. Weston this morning, and at the end of them he gave me a brief account of what had happened."

Emma's blushes, of course, express the mortification she owes to her own erring judgment, as well as her suddenly revived suspicion about Mr. Knightley's feeling toward Harriet; but he interprets them as indications of her distress at being, as he fears, thrown over by Frank Churchill. The tension engendered by this mutual misunderstanding is wound up still further until Mr. Knightley is led to express his solicitude for Emma's wounded feelings and his contempt for what appears to him as Frank's caddish behavior. Emma now understands him and is constrained to disabuse him about the state of her own feelings:

> "Mr. Knightley," said Emma, trying to be lively, but really confused—"I am in a very extraordinary situation. I cannot let you continue in your error; and yet, perhaps, since my manners gave such an impression, I have as much reason to be ashamed of confessing that I never have been at all attached to the person we are speaking of, as it might be natural for a woman to feel in confessing exactly the reverse.—But I never have."
>
> He listened in perfect silence.

Emma takes this silence as implying censure for her own conduct and plunges into a further effort, not to excuse, but to explain it, concluding that she was "somehow or other safe from him." Emma does not yet realize, but perhaps Mr. Knightley has begun to, that her safety lay in the fact that her affections were unknowingly bestowed elsewhere. His silence here is occasioned by the necessity of rearranging his thoughts about Frank Churchill and, more importantly, about his own relation to Emma. Diffidently he edges toward the latter subject by declaring his envy of Frank, but Emma, fearful that they are now "within half a sentence of Harriet," resolves to change the subject. Mr. Knightley breaks out:

> "You will not ask me what is the point of envy.—You are determined, I see, to have no curiosity.—You are wise—but *I* cannot be wise. Emma, I must tell you what you will not ask, though I may wish it unsaid the next moment."
>
> "Oh! then don't speak it, don't speak it," she eagerly cried. "Take a little time, consider, do not commit yourself."
>
> "Thank you," said he, in an accent of deep mortification, and not another syllable followed.

Neither understands the other, and both fear what they imagine they are about to hear. But Emma is instantly contrite at having wounded his feelings and resolves to hear him out at whatever pain to herself:

> "I stopped you ungraciously, just now, Mr. Knightley, and, I am afraid, gave you pain.—But if you have any wish to speakly openly to me as a friend, or to ask my opinion of any thing that you may have in contemplation—as a friend, indeed, you may command me.—I will hear whatever you like. I will tell you exactly what I think."
>
> "As a friend!"—repeated Mr. Knightley.—"Emma, that I fear is a word—No, I have no wish—Stay, yes, why should I hesitate?—I have gone too far already for concealment.—Emma, I accept your offer—Extraordinary as it may seem, I accept it, and refer myself to you as a friend.—Tell me, then, have I no chance of ever succeeding?"

The misunderstandings are at last at an end; Emma and Mr. Knightley have finally arrived at a common plane of intelligence; the complicated fugue has ended. Anything further would be tame and anticlimactic, so we need not be indulged with Emma's reply to Mr. Knightley's professions: "What did she say?—Just what she ought, of course. A lady always does."

That Jane Austen is far more interested in the preliminaries than in the declaration may be taken as evidence that she feels herself unequal to the representation of strong feeling, and certainly her normal practice is to provide even less of the overt language of passion than what she thinks necessary in *Emma*.

Lovers are rarely suffered to declare themselves aloud, and though we hear many articulate refusals we get no equally vehement speeches of acceptance. Charlotte Brontë, for one, could find little evidence of spontaneous feeling in Jane Austen and accordingly assigns her an inferior rank as a novelist: "Miss Austen being . . . without 'sentiment,' without *poetry*, maybe *is* sensible, real (more *real* than *true*), but she cannot be great."[11] But that Jane Austen's novels are deficient in the representation of feeling is simply not true; one must not mistake, as Marianne Dashwood does, the expression for the experience of passion. The tumultuous and conflicting feelings of Emma and Mr. Knightley in the passage just examined are as vividly represented as if they had been overtly stated. Charlotte Brontë's well-known metaphor of the "carefully-fenced, high-cultivated garden, with neat borders and delicate flowers" (II, 43) is no nearer the mark than Harold Nicolson's "neat and maidenly work basket." Why must they insist so on neatness? No one can render better than Jane Austen the confused agitation of contending, often destructive passions, and it should not be hard to think of a better image for confused agitation than "neat borders," or for destructive passions than "delicate flowers."

In the range, variety, complexity, vividness, and even the intensity of the human passions which Jane Austen is capable of representing she is incomparably Charlotte Brontë's superior. If there is a reason for supposing that Charlotte Brontë's awareness of human passion is greater than Jane Austen's, it is that her characters, again like Marianne Dashwood, are so fond of contemplating their own psyches and marveling at the purity and grandeur of their own emotions. Jane Austen's reputation for being deficient in the representation of feeling owes something to her technique of understatement, of expressing rather less than her words actually convey, but still more to what is for her an article of faith as strong as the belief that marrying without love is wrong—that passions, or at least their display, should be kept under control. Marianne is not to be censured for the violence of her feelings but for the egotism that feeds on their indulgence. The true Austen heroine has a better resource when the agitation of her feelings threatens her composure; she plunges into the shrubbery and walks herself calm, far from the eyes of others. It is hardly fair to suppose, however, that success in controlling passion proves the weakness of that passion. Blake testifies to the superiority of energy to reason in a famous aphorism: "Those who restrain desire, do so because theirs is weak enough to be restrained." To this perfect tautology Jane Austen might have responded with an equally circular (and equally incontrovertible) one: "Those who fail to restrain desire, do so because their wills are too weak to exercise restraint." The measure of passion is precisely equal to the measure of restraint which is needed to contain it.

Jane Austen's novels are the product of two converging forces, two fundamental energies. In the first place, the novels grow out of an alert and volatile intelligence which is observant of detail as well as quick to seize upon incongruity wherever it appears but which is at the same time modified by an essentially serious and conventional habit of thought, expressing itself most characteristically in aphorisms and moral *sententiae*. In the second place, the novels employ a consciously evolved technique based on the principle of presenting to the reader only the surface of characters and events which have been much more fully and deeply imagined. The most striking feature of the letters, when one turns to them from the novels, is not, I think, that they reveal a mind wholly alien to the one which conceived the novels, but that they reveal precisely those qualities of mind which can be traced in the novels—the same habit of close observation; the same impulsive tendency to seize on whatever is ridiculous in its range of observation, even at the expense of decorum; the same conservative moral values; the same universalizing and sententious movement of thought. What is strikingly absent from the letters is the technique which controls and disciplines the substance of the novels. The observations of the letters are not subsumed under a unifying vision of life except insofar as some consensus is implicit in the very intimacy subsisting between the two sisters. In the novels Jane Austen was constrained to develop and project some imaginative wholeness, some integrating view of life to organize and energize their manifold details. The letters are slacker precisely because they are directed to a correspondent whose view of life is perfectly known and entirely shared.

I should be sorry if the tendency of my argument were to diminish Jane Austen's stature as a novelist, but I do not think it does. It is certainly no disparagement of her art to affirm that it has its roots in the ordinary concerns of daily life or that it is the product of a rational and intelligible imaginative process. To see that art as mysteriously achieved, either through transcendental visions or abstract intellectual power, is ultimately to devalue it. To see it as humanly inspired and humanly achieved by means of an imaginative power which is unfathomable only in the degree of its intensity is to offer the highest praise.

NOTES

1. R. W. Chapman, ed., *Jane Austen's Letters to Her Sister Cassandra and Others* (Oxford: Clarendon Press, 1932); Harold Nicholson, untitled review, *New Statesman and Nation*, 4 (1932), 659; [E. M. Forster], "Miss Austen and Jane Austen," *Times Literary Supplement*, 10 Nov. 1932, pp. 821-822. Cf. H. W. Garrod: "Her letters may be described as a desert of trivialities punctuated by occasional oases of clever malice" ("Jane Austen: A Depreciation," *Essays by Divers Hands* [London: Oxford University Press, 1928], pp. 21-40).

2. Chapman offers a dignified and pained remonstrance: "There are in fact very few officers at these balls, and I recall nothing that can fairly be called a giggle" (*Jane Austen: Facts and Problems* [Oxford: Clarendon Press, 1948], p. 107).

3. *Marianne Thornton: A Domestic Biography, 1797-1887* (New York: Harcourt, Brace, 1956), p. 4.

4. D. W. Harding in "Regulated Hatred: An Aspect of the Work of Jane Austen," *Scrutiny*, 8 (1940), 346-362, offers a number of examples besides this one.

5. I made this distinction in *The Shaping Vision: Imagination in the English Novel from Defoe to Dickens* (Ithaca: Cornell University Press, 1966), pp. 157-158.

6. I do not wish to weary the reader with superfluous examples, but perhaps the following list (by no means an exhaustive one) will help to suggest how inveterate is Jane Austen's tendency toward sententious utterances. Aphorisms: *SS*, 248-249; *PP*, 236, 237; *MP*, 398, 399, 443, 464; *E*, 17, 144, 165, 181, 320, 482; *NA*, 73, 74, 110-111; *P*, 5, 15, 33, 187. Other moral or philosophical reflections: *SS*, 215, 313, 331, 357; *PP*, 122, 126, 250, 279, 312, 387; *MP*, 2, 201, 234-235, 324, 367, 425, 473; *E*, 97, 112, 117, 137, 231, 271, 431; *NA*, 15, 16, 29-30, 48, 50, 53, 65, 74, 200, 252; *P*, 55, 101, 154, 248, 249.

7. Recent scholarship has tended to show that the range of her observation is much broader than has generally been supposed. See, for example, work by David Daiches, Alistair Duckworth, Avrom Fleishman, Donald Greene, Ward Hellstrom, Arnold Kettle, Tony Tanner, and Lionel Trilling.

8. "The Art of Fiction," *Partial Portraits* (London: Macmillan, 1888), pp. 388-389.

9. J. E. Austen Leigh, *A Memoir of Jane Austen* (London: Richard Bentley, 1883), pp. 148-149.

10. "Jane Austen," *The Common Reader* (New York: Harcourt, Brace, 1925), pp. 196-197.

11. Elizabeth C. Gaskell, *The Life of Charlotte Brontë* (New York: Appleton, 1868), II, 45.

JOEL WEINSHEIMER

JANE AUSTEN'S ANTHROPOCENTRISM

Among Jane Austen's reflections on her own novels, none is more important than that in which she evaluates *Pride and Prejudice:*

> The work is rather too light, and bright, and sparkling; it wants shade; it wants to be stretched out here and there with a long chapter of sense, if it could be had; if not, of solemn specious nonsense, about something unconnected with the story, an essay on writing, a critique on Walter Scott, or the history of Buonaparté, or anything that would form a contrast, and bring the reader with increased delight to the playfulness and epigrammatism of the general style. (*Letters,* 299-300)

There is substantial agreement that, besides describing her most popular novel, Jane Austen here anticipates a tonal and thematic shift toward solemnity in *Mansfield Park.* But broader significance can be found in these self-critical remarks if we examine what I take to be their central phrase. *Pride and Prejudice,* Jane Austen writes, lacks a "long chapter of sense" or even of "nonsense," but whatever such a chapter would contain, its subject must be "something unconnected with the story." It could be something prosy and abstract, such as "an essay on writing, a critique on Walter Scott," or on the other hand it could be something concrete and actual but outside the immediate concerns of the characters, such as "the history of Buonaparté." For an essay on writing in a novel we could go to *Tom Jones* or more recently Joyce's *Portrait;* for a history of Bonaparte our range is much greater. The fact that *Pride and Prejudice* includes no such chronicle seems hardly worth our attention until we recall how many excellent novels, including what is generally conceded to be the greatest novel, contain precisely that—histories of Napoleon and the French Revolution. Dickens, Thackeray, Hugo, and of course Tolstoy, to name the most important, each found an epic subject in the period of world history spanned by Jane Austen's lifetime. She was fourteen years old at the storming of the Bastille, twenty-four when Napoleon came to power, and forty at the time of Waterloo, two years before her death. A metaphysical as well as a physical war, the French Revolution and its aftermath virtually seduced greater and lesser novelists alike into fictionalizing it, but Jane Austen remained inviolate.

It would be crude to condemn Jane Austen outright for the absence, however conspicuous, of Napoleon in her novels. Yet this lack seems to underlie a charge that has been levelled against her since her first published novels began to establish a pattern. Especially since the completion of Chapman's edition of the major novels in the early 1930s, Jane Austen has risen quickly in her readers' estimation. Yet there has persisted a trickle of discontent sufficient to make her appreciators wary of praising her unreservedly. The growth of Jane Austen's reputation has been impeded by nagging, often covert, imputations that she is somehow "limited"—limited in scope, in passion, in action, in social and historical consciousness, and ultimately in value.

I need not take time here to survey the history of her detractors; from Charlotte Brontë to Angus Wilson, they are familiar enough. Nevertheless it is important to remind ourselves that the charge of limitations is longstanding and cannot be easily dismissed, for in literary criticism the longevity of an opinion is our best indicator of its truth. We are in no position to lament the persisting ignorance of Twain, Trollope, James, Conrad, Lawrence, and others whose credentials justify attention to their detractions. This is certainly not to say that each of the deficiencies ascribed to Jane Austen during the past century and a half is equally valid; rather I would point out that the question of her limitations is at bottom a question of judicial criticism and one that therefore requires at least a modicum of agreement if our discussion is to have any validity at all. Many qualified readers have found Jane Austen's novels wanting, and this is the closest to objectivity that the inexact science of literary assessment can approach. But though there is sufficient agreement to suggest that she is somehow deficient, there is none to specify in what way. If we concurred with all of the objections raised by our predecessors, Jane Austen would be reduced to an awkward, amoral trifler. This conclusion is clearly untenable. Our specification of Jane Austen's deficiencies must be proportionate to the excellences she manifestly possesses. The limitations we discern must be such as do not constrict her absolutely. If we are to discover Jane Austen's imperfections, I propose looking for them where she pointed—in "something unconnected with the story."

We should begin with the premise that Jane Austen is a conscious artist—conscious of the tradition in which she wrote and of her individual artistry. There is nothing mechanical about her novels; each word is deliberately chosen to fulfill a precise rhetorical intention. Likewise her limitations of subject are conscious and deliberately self-imposed. They constitute in themselves meaningful thematic statements. Once we acknowledge the deliberateness of Jane Austen's self-restriction, we can sense that the charge of limitation is misdirected when it takes the form of a mere complaint that she has not enough of sex, death, the poor, or whatever. An artist may exclude anything he wishes, so long as that exclusion does not ultimately distort or devalue his subject. But even in denying the validity of such complaints I am assuming that the value of a work of art does depend partly on the importance of its subject, that subjects can vary in importance, and that the techniques which confer importance can be described and defined. In short, I am assuming that overt judgment can be legitimate. By examining Jane Austen's treatment of the physical world, the metaphysical world, and the implications of these two for the moral world, we can investigate her conception of man's nature and predicament within the limits she prescribes and, just as objectively, we can judge the accuracy and completeness of that conception. First, then, the physical world.

Jane Austen's concern for the economics of marriage—for dowries, settlements, inheritances, the equalization of monetary claims—combined with her ridicule of the romanticization of poverty has led some readers, notably David Daiches and Mark Schorer, to discover in her works a vein of materialism. And we cannot deny that money is of great, though not exclusive, importance to Jane Austen and her characters. In this confined sense, she is a materialist. But if we expand our definition of the material to include things in her novels, natural and artificial things to be seen, touched, discussed, and used—in fact, if we extend our idea of the material to comprehend the physical generally—it becomes clear that Jane Austen is something far other than a materialist.

In reading Jane Austen's best novels, we do not feel that her characters lack specificity or concreteness; we are introduced to people rather than types. But it is noteworthy that in particularizing her characters, contrary to her meticulously detailed psychological and moral verisimilitude, Jane Austen generally avoids physical minutiae.[1] Emma's high cheekbones and aquiline nose, for instance, exist only in the reader's imagination. Emma is "handsome," and we are told very little more. Similarly, Mrs. Musgrove's corpulence is brought up only to be dismissed as morally irrelevant, and the details of Mrs. Elton's ball dress are inserted to excite ridicule of her ostentation and only incidentally to assist the reader in visualizing her. There is wide agreement that sound artistic principles justify Jane Austen's minimizing the details of appearance. We know first that the omission was deliberate. A passage in the letters makes clear that she imagined her heroines very particularly. At a painting exhibition in 1813, Jane Austen found "a small portrait of Mrs. Bingley, excessively like her. I went in hopes of seeing one of her Sister, but there was no Mrs. Darcy;—perhaps however, I may find her in the Great Exhibition. . . . Mrs. Bingley's is exactly herself, size, shaped face, features & sweetness; there never was a greater likeness. She is dressed in a white gown, with green ornaments, which convinces me of what I had always supposed, that green was a favourite colour with her. I dare say Mrs. D. will be in Yellow" (*Letters*, 309-310). These details are omitted from the novel because Jane Austen felt that overparticularization of any kind was effeminate or, worse, dull. Such detailing is a quality later associated with Harriet Smith, Miss Bates, and the boorish Mrs. Elton—not Emma. Most important though among the reasons for minimizing physical appearance is that Jane Austen retained a faith in the validity of generalization, and this artistic faith encouraged her to express a complex of particulars by a single general attribute. Her exclusions in respect to the details of personal appearance are indeed defensible, and we cannot hastily assign them any aesthetic demerits.

Nor should we deduce any ready conclusions from the relative absence of the physical as represented by nature in her works. "You describe a sweet place," Jane Austen writes to her niece Anna, the fledgling novelist, "but your descriptions are often more minute than will be liked. You give too many particulars of right hand & left" (*Letters*, 401). Jane Austen's own sweet scenes on the ramparts at Portsmouth or at Lyme Regis are memorably described, but these are striking precisely because such detailing of natural scenes is exceptional. Jane Austen's is largely an indoor world, where civilized gentlemen and women are defended from snow, heat, rain, and other inclemencies that threaten health and decorum. When her characters do venture outside, they walk in parks and gardens fashioned for protection from the chaos that lurks in the wilderness. But whether presented as enjoyment or discomfort, nature remains human-oriented. Rarely are natural scenes presented uncolored by the mind of the observer or untouched by the hand of the landscaper. But almost no one regrets that Jane Austen has not more of the picturesque; we can dispense with rocky craigs, lofty heights, and undulating meadows. The relative absence of nature in the novels is not of itself an artistic deficiency.[2]

Similarly, if we consider the physical as represented by the relatively few concrete objects that enter the novels—the mud on Elizabeth's petticoat, Wentworth's homiletic nut, or the watch Sir Thomas Bertram consults so religiously—it becomes clear that these objects are strategically placed primarily for the purpose of characterization. Mr. Woodhouse's bowl of gruel is presented not as a mere object but as an expression, even an extension, of his valetudinarianism. When we look into the mirrors of Kellynch Hall and see there the image of Sir Walter Elliot, we begin to realize that things in Jane Austen's novels are humanized. By this I do not mean that they are personified but rather that objects accumulate moral value by their intimacy with people. So strictly does Jane Austen focus on men and women that the physical, the nonhuman, is subordinated to and ultimately assimilated into the human. Objects tend to lose their palpability as inscrutable, alien substances and instead become projections of a character's personality. So closely is the sofa identified with Lady Bertram's indolence or the library with Mr. Bennet's irresponsibility that the very condemnation implied is almost comfortable. Objects in the novels are like much-worn clothes: whether shabby or elegant, they have taken the form of their owners.

Having visited two exhibitions shortly before revising *First Impressions*, Jane reported to her sister, "I had some amusement at each, tho' my preference for Men & Women, always inclines me to attend more to the company than the sight" (*Letters*, 267). Perhaps, I suggest, attention to the sight, attention to autonomous physical reality, is part of the "something unconnected with the story" of men and women missing from *Pride and Prejudice*. In Dickens's *Our Mutual Friend*, where this attention to the autonomy of things is present, the pure upper Thames promises regeneration whereas the lower river threatens man with absorption into its primeval slime. But it is possible for the Thames to save or damn only because of its inhumanity. Perhaps what we lack in reading Jane Austen is a chapter on whales, one that would establish the otherness of things, their primal indifference to human feelings and judgments. Without requiring that we be confronted with an existential doorknob like that in Sartre's *Nausea* or a Camusian tundra "where nothing had any connection with man," we can nevertheless desire a novelistic world in which we are somewhat less benevolently comforted by objects that silently hymn man's self-importance. The irony that results from humanizing things is that while Jane Austen deflates mankind's capacity for particular acts of kindness and understanding, she inflates man's general self-esteem by neglecting to contextualize him in a sphere of reference larger than himself. The scant details of her characters' physical appearance, the few natural scenes she presents, the few independent objects, each serves to remind us, by their very scarcity, not merely that the proper study of mankind is man. Jane Austen's treatment of the physical implies that mankind cannot be defined in relation to anything but itself.

The Jane Austen of the novels, I have suggested, is not a materialist in the wider sense of the word. But neither is she an immaterialist; Jane Austen propounds no ideas that antecede their manifestation in personal relations. Of itself this absence of general ideas is certainly no defect. On the contrary, Northrop Frye asserts, the "interest in ideas and theoretical statements is alien to the genius of the novel proper, where the technical problem is to dissolve all theory into personal relationships. In Jane Austen, to take a familiar instance, church, state, and culture are never examined except as social data."[3] Virginia Woolf comes to much the same conclusion when she writes that in Jane Austen "nothing happens . . . for its own oddity or curiosity but with relation to something else. No avenues of suggestion are opened up, no doors are suddenly flung wide; the ropes which tighten the structure, since they are all rooted in the heart, are so held firmly and tightly. For, in order to develop personal relations to the utmost, it is important to keep out of the range of the abstract, the impersonal; and to suggest that there is anything that lies outside men and women would be to cast the shadow of doubt upon the comedy of their relationships and its sufficiency."[4] Woolf raises the problem of the impersonal and praises Jane Austen for circumventing it. We too can agree that ideological preachments are needless. Nevertheless Jane Austen's modest refusal to lead the reader through personal experience to the glimpse of a larger, impersonal truth constricts both her technique and the overall import of her art.

We are familiar with E. M. Forster's distinction between flat and round characters. Less well known is his third category of character, which he calls "prophetic song," an awkward term that has not attained critical currency. "Song" can best be explained as a second kind of flatness, a category of characters who retain their complex and discrete personality and yet approach the clarity and simplicity of an impersonal idea. Melville's Ahab achieves this simplicity by virtue of his monomania; Forster's own Professor Godbole becomes impersonal by his very characterlessness. But Dostoevsky best illustrates this second flatness. His fictions are populated by credible types, characters who are individuals and yet participate in and reflect an idea that exists independent of its embodiment in themselves. Readers of *The Idiot,* for example, are invited to believe that Prince Mishkin is not a madman nor even an altruist; rather he is an imperfect but clear emanation of an autonomous, divine idea. For this reason, the idea does not reflect Prince Mishkin; it is not tainted by his foibles and peculiarities. Instead he reflects the idea; his faults are lessened by its perfection. In explaining Dostoevsky's "song" Forster contrasts *Mansfield Park* and *The Brothers Karamazov:* "Lady Bertram sitting on her sofa with pug," he writes, "may assist us in these deeper matters. Lady Bertram, we decided, was a flat character, capable of extending into a round when the action required it. Mitya is a round character, but he is capable of extension. He does not conceal anything (mysticism), he does not mean anything (symbolism), he is merely Dmitri Karamazov, but to be merely a person in Dostoevsky is to join up with all the other people far back. . . . Dostoevsky's characters ask us to share something deeper than their experiences."[5]

Jane Austen, intentionally I think, avoids this kind of typological character. Those of her people who approach simplicity do so through self-caricature; deficiencies of intelligence or charity distinguish their peculiar personalities.[6] Unlike the allegorical flatness that signifies generality, the flatness of Jane Austen's flat characters emphasizes their particularity as discrete individuals. Likewise we experience the heroines of the mature novels as very specific, though not aberrant, women. When Mr. Knightley describes Emma's fate as "the fate of thousands," the reader remains unconvinced that her unique maturation represents either the experience of young women in general or the ideal to which they aspire. Jane Austen's characters are, as Forster says, "round or capable of rotundity," but they are not capable of the flatness of song. Unlike Dostoevsky's, her characters are the terminus of novelistic investigation, not media of impersonal ideas visible through them. For Jane Austen, people cannot be allegorical, symbolic, or prophetic either in life or in literature. Here, then, is a second aspect of that "something unconnected with the story" of men and women missing in *Pride and Prejudice*, the absence of impersonal ideas.

That Jane Austen's characters do not participate consciously or unconsciously in such ideas has direct consequences for the concept of education in the novels. It is probably accurate to say that Jane Austen the author recognized no value higher than the knowledge of oneself. We need look no further than the triangle of Fanny, Edmund, and Mary Crawford to see that their creator categorized and ranked her characters by their degree of self-knowledge. But self-knowledge varies in kind as well as degree, and that variety which Jane Austen upholds may prove a less comprehensive standard than we could wish. "For the Austen character," Kenneth Moler writes, "self-knowledge entails not the scanning of the universe's mysteries but 'knowledge of the heart,' of the 'tendencies of his soul,' of his human fallibility and of the particular directions in which, as an individual, he has erred and is likely to err in the complex business of the moral life. . . . And in Emma Woodhouse's moments of crisis we find Jane Austen's heroine, not asking, 'Who am I? Why was I born? What does it all mean?' but examining her tendency to a particular evil."[7] Moler correctly emphasizes the heroine's recognition of her general fallibility and specific errors as a remedy for self-ignorance. But to say that Emma either seeks or finds evil in herself is mistaken, for Jane Austen consistently refrains from investigating the abstract moral systems by which her heroine's particular defects of self-knowledge can be defined as sins.

Emma, to retain Moler's example, dramatizes the sources and effects of pride: the proud deceive themselves and harm others. Further, the novel shows that pride is a corrigible quality which leaves no taint after its correction; the intelligent characters are undeceived and the harm rectified. But to define pride as a species of ignorance, a disposition misdirected by the mere lack of knowledge, is to circumscribe this moral offense within the province of personal and social error. In Richard Simpson's words, "Miss Austen has a most Platonic inclination to explain away knavishness into folly."[8] Hence when Mark Schorer contends that the problem of *Emma* is "nothing less than original sin,"[9] such inflation of the novel's moral import is unconvincing. Jane Austen provides no frame of ideas by which pride can be more than an antisocial defect of character. Emma's pride is examined strictly within the confines of its human origins and human victims, and though we recognize the seriousness of errors that demean oneself and hurt others, we find no admission on Jane Austen's part that pride is either sin or evil. It is a quality of human thought and action not a participation with an impersonal idea. This lack of an impersonal frame of ideas by which to raise error to the level of evil occasions the most damaging criticism that can be levelled against Jane Austen—that she is a novelist of manners.

I have argued that Jane Austen can be properly termed neither a materialist nor an immaterialist. At this point it is tempting to retreat to some honorific term, such as realism or classicism, with which to resolve the opposition in a comfortable obscurity. But the middle ground that Jane Austen occupies is not so easily described. To lack either a view of things or ideas as extrinsic to human concerns is not of itself a defect. However, such a lack is not a mere gap in Jane Austen's comprehensiveness to be lamented in passing or explained away. The strict dependence of the material and the immaterial on the human directly affects her portrayal of man's nature and condition. Specifically, Jane Austen focuses so exclusively on men, on their social and moral relations to themselves and their fellows, that she severely circumscribes her conception of what men are.

As I perceive it, the central defect of Jane Austen's novels is that they study man in a vacuum. Something unconnected with the story of men and women is not there; that something is the not-man. Since otherwise autonomous things and ideas are humanized in her works, the nonhuman toward which men tend at their best and worst is all but eliminated. Jane Austen offers us pathos but not tragedy, comedy but not divine comedy, because she posits only the human, only one level of being, as the sole reality. Her characters inhabit a middle world not because they follow the mean but because no other world is real. Neither her fools, villains, heroes, nor heroines can so degrade or elevate themselves that they become thinglike; none participate in a positive or negative impersonal ideal. Instead they are imprisoned within their own humanity. Consequently the importance of restraint, continence, and self-discipline is reduced in proportion to the characters' reduced capacities; and when the author circumscribes the possibility of man's extending himself and thereby devalues the necessity of limiting himself, the reader's sense of moral urgency is measurably diminished.

Human and therefore aesthetic importance is finally relative, that is to say, it consists in relation. The experience of Jane Austen's heroines achieves its great significance relative to her potential self, relative to her paternal and marital family, relative to her society and to the human community of which we and the author are members, but that is where its significance ends. Ironically, by so aggrandizing men and women that they become the exclusive subject of the novels, Jane Austen limits their importance. For just as individual importance is defeated by Narcissism, so also is collective human importance limited by anthropocentrism. Considered as an isolated subject, the moral and social relations of men and women are indeed important, but it is the nonhuman context of human experience that confers on it the greatest significance. Because Jane Austen refrains from exploring the nonhuman realities which separated from man give him definition and connected give him grandeur, her characters are divested of part of their human potential. Thus it is not the "two inches of Ivory" or the "3 or 4 Families in a Country Village" or the absence of Napoleon that constitutes Jane Austen's limitations; her novels seem small because her characters, the focal components of her vision, achieve less than the fullest humanity.

Let other pens dwell on imperfection. I quit such odious subjects as soon as I can. The danger of depreciation is that it will be confused (by author or reader) with damnation, but this essay attempts no more than to place Jane Austen in a hierarchy of excellence. And though it concludes that she does not stand at the apex of the best practitioners of the novel, she nevertheless belongs among them. Finally I would associate this assessment of Jane Austen with that of George Lewes: "Her fame, as we think, must endure. Such art as hers can never grow old, never be superseded. But, after all, miniatures are not frescoes, and her works are miniatures. Her place is among the Immortals; but the pedestal is erected in a quiet niche of the great temple" (Southam, p. 166).

NOTES

1. Table II-1 in Karl Kroeber's *Styles in Fictional Structure* (Princeton: Princeton University Press, 1971), p. 209, shows that among Austen, Dickens, Charlotte Brontë, and Eliot, Jane Austen has the smallest ratio of "words referring to parts of the body and bodily movement." Such words occur in Dickens five times more often.

2. See Lord David Cecil, "A Note on Jane Austen's Scenery," *The Fine Art of Reading* (Indianapolis: Bobbs-Merrill, 1957), pp. 161-175, and Margaret Lane, "Jane Austen's Sleight-of-Hand," *Purely for Pleasure* (New York: Knopf, 1967), pp. 111-125. Both agree that, whether Jane Austen was describing outside scenes or domestic interiors, she limited herself to few physical details and only those relevant to characterization.

3. *Anatomy of Criticism: Four Essays* (1957; rpt. New York: Atheneum, 1968), p. 308.

4. "Phases of Fiction" (1929), *Granite and Rainbow* (New York: Harcourt, Brace, 1958), p. 115.

5. *Aspects of the Novel* (1927; rpt. New York: Harcourt, Brace and World, 1955), p. 134. It is probably in this contrast of the two novelists that we should look for an explanation of Forster's comment that he "learned the possibilities of domestic humor" from Jane Austen; "I was more ambitious than she was, of course; I tried to hitch it on to other things" (*Paris Review*, no. 1 [1953], p. 39).

6. I would note the exception of Jane Bennet, who uniquely achieves simplicity and yet avoids simplemindedness.

7. *Jane Austen's Art of Allusion* (Lincoln: University of Nebraska Press, 1968), p. 9.

8. In *Jane Austen: The Critical Heritage*, ed. B. C. Southam (New York: Barnes and Noble, 1968), p. 249. In "*Mansfield Park:* Three Problems," *Nineteenth-Century Fiction*, 29 (1974), 185-205, I have examined more particularly the questions raised by Simpson's statement.

9. "The Humiliation of Emma Woodhouse," *Literary Review*, 2 (1959), 563.

DONALD GREENE

THE MYTH OF LIMITATION

I

There is no difficulty in finding material for a study of the charge of "limitation" against Jane Austen. It is the one steady landmark in the swirling waters of Jane Austen criticism, the security blanket to which the critic who is vaguely aware of her greatness but doesn't quite know why, or the critic who can't see what all the shouting is about, desperately clings. There seems little point in attempting a systematic history of the use of this shibboleth—almost everyone who writes on her (there are a very few distinguished exceptions)[1] displays a compulsive need to make use of that blessed word sooner or later, usually sooner.

So for my texts I have merely pulled down at random a few well-known books on the novel. Arnold Kettle writes,

> The silliest of all criticisms of Jane Austen is the one which blames her for not writing about the Battle of Waterloo and the French Revolution. She wrote about what she understood and no artist can do more. But did she understand enough? . . . The limitation and the narrowness of the Hartfield world is the limitation of class society. . . . The values and standards of the Hartfield world are based on the assumption that it is right and proper for a minority of the community to live at the expense of the majority. . . . Now this charge, that the value of *Emma* is seriously lim-

> ited by the class basis of Jane Austen's standards, cannot be ignored or written off as a non-literary issue. If the basic interest of the novel is indeed a moral interest, then it can scarcely be considered irrelevant to face the question that the standards we are called upon to admire may be inseparably linked with a particular form of social organization.[2]

This expression of the popular "class limitation" variety of the charge immediately brings a number of questions to the mind. The implication seems to be that a novel about the Battle of Waterloo or the French Revolution is ipso facto a better novel than one about Hartfield–surely a dubious assumption. And this in turn raises the basic question of just what the function of the novel is, a question to which we shall later return. Anyway, how do we know that Jane Austen did not understand the French Revolution and the Napoleonic War–she lost a relation to the guillotine in the first and had two brothers on active service for many years in the second–as well as Tolstoy, say, who was not born until they were over, or as Arnold Kettle? Indeed, how many even of specialist historians of those events would have the chutzpah to say that they fully "understood" them? And if one of them did so believe, would he not be better occupied in incorporating his understanding in a history than in a novel? In how many ages and regions of the world has there *not* been a "class society"? Are the works of Homer and Sophocles and Shakespeare similarly vitiated by the limitation that they lived in and wrote about one? Did, in fact, the minority of the Hartfield–rather, Highbury–community live at the expense of the majority? Mr. Knightley, like Mr. Darcy and Sir Thomas Bertram in other novels, owned a considerable estate and no doubt spent much of his time managing it–"improving it," as the title of a recent book on Jane Austen puts it–supervising his tenants, farm-laborers, and so on, and as a consequence lived in greater material comfort than they. But one understands that even in Soviet Russia commissars have substantially more perquisites and privileges than the workmen they supervise, in recognition of their administrative skills.

Anyway, how does the fact that Jane Austen depicts in her novels the "class society" that she lived in demonstrate the "class basis" of her "standards" or that she calls on us to admire the standards of that society? I would maintain, on the contrary, that her standards, her moral values, have no class basis whatever. She values honesty, decency, clear-sightedness, emotional responsiveness in whatever class they occur: her most contemptible characters—Lady Catherine de Bourgh, Sir Walter Elliot, General Tilney—are often the highest in the scale of wealth and social prestige.

Another variety of the charge of limitation is presented by Lionel Stevenson. "The absence of passion is a graver limitation, since the dominant theme of all her novels is love. She is so suspicious of emotion that when a scene of strong feeling is imperative she tries to avoid narrating it. . . . Of the sixteen kisses mentioned in the novels, not one is exchanged by a pair of lovers. Her heroines are so sensible and self-controlled that even in their secret thoughts they do not allow sex to intrude."[3] Stevenson's statistical assiduity is to be admired. One wishes he had gone on to count the number of explicit descriptions of kisses of passion between hero and heroine in the works of those robust, uninhibited male novelists, Scott, Dickens, and Thackeray. Offhand, I can't recollect a single one—perhaps the occasional chaste brushing of the lips against the cheek or forehead of an Agnes or Amelia. And how does Stevenson know what went on in the secret thoughts of Jane Austen's heroines—or for that matter Shakespeare's Rosalind, Portia, or Beatrice? She leaves us in no doubt as to what went on in the secret thoughts of some other women characters, thoughts that were fully acted out by Lydia Bennet, Maria Rushworth, Mrs. Clay, for instance—thoughts in which sex very clearly "intruded."

Stevenson seems to be using the terms *passion* and *emotion* and *feeling* in a highly technical—indeed, "limited"—sense, the sense they began to acquire about the time of Elinor Glyn, who initiated the practice of titillating the prurience of the mass readership of best sellers by fairly explicit accounts of sexual intercourse; and who will argue that the novel has improved as a result of this development? What an incredible thing to say, after all, that Jane Austen avoids narrating "scenes of strong feeling"! Can Stevenson never have read chapter 34 of *Pride and Prejudice* or chapter 46 of *Sense and Sensibility* or chapter 43 of *Emma*? By any normal use of the term Elizabeth Bennet is a passionate person; so is Darcy; and Jane Austen so deftly presents their personalities that—in case anyone is still worrying about this matter—she leaves me, at any rate, in no doubt that after their marriage they had quite as good a time in bed as Lydia and Wickham; probably better, for, by comparison with Darcy, Wickham is a pretty cold fish.

And Dorothy Van Ghent sums it up in omnibus fashion: "It is the frequent response of readers who are making their first acquaintance with Jane Austen that her subject matter is itself so limited—limited to the manners of a small section of English country gentry, who apparently never have been worried about death or sex, hunger or war, guilt or God—that it can offer no contiguity with modern interests. This is a very real difficulty in an approach to an Austen novel, and we should not obscure it."[4] I began thinking over this list of the six ingredients Professor Van Ghent felt it necessary for a novel to contain in order for it to provide "contiguity"—a nice euphemism for "relevance"—"with modern interests": death, sex, hunger, war, guilt, God. When I cast around in my memory for a modern novel that would eminently qualify, the first that came to my mind was, for some reason, James Jones's *From Here to Eternity*, now so thoroughly forgotten, though it is only a little over twenty years ago that it was the great best-seller of the time and the great movie a little later. It had death; it had sadism; it had hunger—at least it contained large chunks of "social consciousness," which I suppose is what is meant. It had sex—how thrilled we all were at the daring of the famous copulation scene on the Hawaiian beach! It had war—the attack on Pearl Harbor, no less. Indeed it combined the last two ingredients in a short sentence of priceless felicity, to which Jane Austen could never have hoped to aspire: "Pearl Harbor made a queasiness in the testicles." To be sure, the characters in Jones's book are not much more worried about God than were the English country gentry of the late eighteenth century. But then the number of novels, in any time or place, in which God plays a very large part is small. One has, of course, to except those of Tolstoy and Dostoevsky, though I am not sure that it is for His role in them that most readers find them memorable.

But I still find that Jane Austen's novels offer at least as much "contiguity with modern interests" as Jones's. As usual in such critiques, Professor Van Ghent gives an inaccurate account: she describes the "image" of a Jane Austen novel rather than the reality. The seemingly impending death of a central character forms the climax of one of them: Professor Van Ghent has forgotten the plot of *Sense and Sensibility*, or at least chapters 42 to 47. The death of Fanny Harville accounts for an important subplot in *Persuasion*, as does the near fatal accident of Louisa Musgrove. Fanny Price in *Mansfield Park* worries about the possible death in action of her brother, and in *Persuasion* the theme of death at sea runs a powerful undertone throughout the novel ("'Ah!' cried Captain Harville, in a tone of strong feeling, 'if I could but make you comprehend what a man suffers when he takes a last look at his wife and children, and watches the boat he has sent them off in, as long as it is in sight, and then turns away and says 'God knows whether we ever meet again!'" (234-235).[5] Illicit sex occurs in all the novels except *Northanger Abbey* and brings about the dénouement of two of them, *Pride and Prejudice* and *Mansfield Park*. Perhaps it is because Jane Austen often takes such matters in her stride that critics overlook them. Not only is Harriet Smith's illegitimacy in *Emma* taken as a matter of course, but Jane Austen can even laugh at "society's" attitude toward it and Emma's romanticizing of it. Harriet turns out in the end to be the child of a tradesman: "Such was the blood of gentility which Emma had formerly been so ready to vouch for! It was likely to be as untainted, perhaps, as the blood of many a gentleman: but what a connection had she been preparing for Mr. Knightley—or for the Churchills—or even for Mr. Elton! The stain of illegitimacy, unbleached by nobility or wealth, would have been a stain indeed" (482).[6] If anyone thinks Jane Austen's tongue is not in her cheek here, he should notice the mention of Mr. Elton and the satiric image "unbleached." (What, by the way, does *untainted* mean? Can she be referring to anything but syphilis?) And there is the notorious account of young Musgrove's death in *Persuasion:* "The Musgroves had had the ill fortune of a very troublesome, hopeless son, and the good fortune to lose him before he reached his twentieth year. . . . He had, in fact, though his sisters were now doing all they could for him, by calling him 'poor Richard,' been nothing better than a thick-headed, unfeeling, unprofitable Dick Musgrove, who had never done anything to entitle himself to more than the abbreviation of his name, living or dead" (50-51). Some readers have held up their hands in horror at the "callousness" of this. Jane Austen can't win, it seems. Either she is characterized as so "limited" that she shudders at the idea of death and sex and cannot bring herself to mention them, or else she is berated for being utterly cynical about them.

As for hunger, one might remember Jane Fairfax on the plight of the young unmarried woman of good birth and education but without financial means:

> "When I am quite determined as to the time, I am not at all afraid of being long unemployed. There are places in town, offices, where inquiry would soon produce some-

> thing—offices for the sale, not quite of human flesh, but of human intellect."
>
> "Oh! my dear, human flesh! You quite shock me; if you mean a fling at the slave-trade, I assure you Mr. Suckling was always rather a friend to the abolition."
>
> "I did not mean—I was not thinking of the slave-trade," replied Jane; "governess-trade, I assure you, was all that I had in view; widely different certainly as to the guilt of those who carry it on; but as to the greater misery of the victims, I do not know where it lies." (*E*, 300-301)

And on war (and government):

> "The Admiralty . . . entertain themselves now and then with sending a few hundred men to sea in a ship not fit to be employed. But they have a great many to provide for; and among the thousands that may just as well go to the bottom as not, it is impossible for them to distinguish the very set who may be least missed." (*P*, 65)

As James Jones might say, this causes a queasiness in the testicles. Captain Wentworth, the speaker, continues with a lively and detailed account of his naval actions in this tub:

> "After taking privateers enough to be very entertaining, I had the good luck in my passage home, the next autumn, to fall in with the very French frigate I wanted. I brought her into Plymouth; and here was another instance of luck. We had not been six hours in the Sound, when a gale came on, which lasted four days and nights, and which would have done for poor old *Asp* in half the time. . . . Four-and-twenty hours later, and I should only have been a gallant Captain Wentworth, in a small paragraph at one corner of the newspapers; and being lost in only a sloop, nobody would have thought about me."
>
> Anne's shudderings were to herself alone. (66)

As for guilt, it is the main staple of the novels. The plot of every one of them turns, as much as any Greek tragedy, on the recognition by one or more of the central characters of guilt and the subsequent self-reproach, self-insight, and reparation. No, Jane Austen understood a very great deal about the darker, the more tragic and sordid aspects of life, and did not hesitate to incorporate them in her novels.

II

Of course, Jane Austen was to some extent herself to blame for this label. She dropped one or two remarks about her own performance which later critics, as the easiest solution, seized on and have repeated again and again with the utmost solemnity and literalness. They tend to forget what a consummate ironist she is. There is the famous, or notorious, "two inches of ivory." It is really time that this phrase, useful as it is to Austenian critics, was put back into context. It occurs in a letter, one of her most charming ones, to her young nephew, James Edward Austen, who has just left school. It is worth the space to quote the opening of it, by way of recapturing the tone of the letter:

> My dear Edward,
>
> One reason for my writing to you now is that I may have the pleasure of directing to you *Esqre*. I give you joy of having left Winchester. Now you may own how miserable you were there; now it will gradually all come out—your crimes and miseries—how often you went up by the mail to London and threw away fifty guineas at a tavern, and how often you were on the point of hanging yourself, restrained only, as some ill-natured aspersion on poor old Winton has it, by the want of a tree within some miles of the city.

A delightful dig at the self-pitying, self-romanticizing, "unhappy schooldays" and "unhappy childhood" tradition, which has been responsible for some good and much dreary autobiography and fiction in English and other languages. It was the heyday of Byronism. In the most engaging way, Aunt Jane is warning the boy, who is at the age when the advice is most needed, "Don't act or think like a character out of popular fiction."

Young Edward has been inspired by his aunt's example to try his hand at novel writing. Jane Austen continues with some family news; then,

> Uncle Henry writes very superior sermons. You and I must try to get hold of one or two, and put them into our novels; it would be a fine help to a volume–

one is sure of what she thinks about novelists who put sermons into their novels to help pad them out (she might have made an exception for Sterne)–

> and we could make our heroine read it aloud of a Sunday evening, just as Isabella Wardour in *The Antiquary* is made to read the history of the Hartz Demon in the ruins of St. Ruth–though I believe, upon recollection, Lovell is the reader.[7]

Nor, clearly, did she approve of long interpolated ghost stories and the like. Jane Austen is somewhat less kind to Scott's novels than he was to hers; which is as it should have been.

Then comes a reference to a mysterious disaster that has occurred to the manuscript of the novel Edward has been working on:

> By the bye, my dear Edward, I am quite concerned for the loss your mother mentions in her letters; two chapters and a half to be missing is monstrous! It is well that *I* have not been at Steventon lately, and therefore cannot be suspected of purloining them–two strong twigs and a half toward a nest of my own would have been something. I do not think however that any theft of that sort would be really very useful to me. What should I do with your strong, manly, spirited sketches, full of variety and glow? How could I possibly join them on to the little bit (two inches wide) of ivory on which I work with so fine a brush as produces little effect? (*Letters*, 467-469)

It must be kept in mind that this is a forty-year-old woman, who has published four highly successful novels, the last dedicated by request to the Prince Regent and recently given a rave review by Sir Walter Scott in the prestigious *Quarterly*, writing to an eighteen-year-old schoolboy. I think the modesty of "two inches of ivory" and "produces little effect" needs to be taken with the same number of grains of salt as the praise of the "strong, manly, spirited sketches, full of variety and glow" of the boy, who did, when he was over seventy, publish an excellently written memoir of his aunt, but never managed to get a novel into print. Rather I detect, under the jocosity, a considerable amount of the proper pride of a serious, mature, successful professional artist—and perhaps even a touch of justified "female chauvinism" in the "manly."[8] She who, without having had a chance to go to Winchester or (as Edward was to do) to Oxford, had beaten the great Sir Walter at his own game was not, I think, really apologizing for the inadequacies, the "limitations" of her work to this young male whippersnapper—especially when the passage occurs in a letter already full of snide comments on the kind of book that Jane Austen does *not* want to write and probably thinks should not be written at all.

Not so often used in evidence against her—indeed it is difficult to do so, so evident is the contempt she holds for the kind of work that has been suggested—is her reply to the Prince Regent's librarian:

> You are very very kind in your hints as to the sort of composition which might recommend me at present, and I am fully sensible that an historical romance, founded on the House of Saxe Cobourg, might be much more to the purpose of profit or popularity than such pictures of domestic life in country villages as I deal in. But I could no more write a romance than an epic poem. I could not sit seriously down to write a serious romance under any other motive than to save my life; and if it were indispensable for me to keep it up and never relax into laughing at myself or

> other people, I am sure I should be hung before I had finished the first chapter. No, I must keep to my own style and go on in my own way; and though I may never succeed again in that, I am convinced that I should totally fail in any other. (*Letters*, 452-453)

I detect no sense of real limitation in her expression of inability to sit "seriously" down to write a "serious" historical romance about the House of Saxe-Cobourg, and I rather think the "laughter" she speaks of is really directed at the idea of such a work and perhaps at "serious historical romances" generally.

Finally, and most damaging, there is the much-cited passage at the beginning of the last chapter of *Mansfield Park:* "Let other pens dwell on guilt and misery. I quit such odious objects as soon as I can" (451). It seems to me astonishing that critics, after exclaiming in pious horror at such voluntary self-limitation, fail to notice that, after Jane Austen has written this, she immediately goes on to dwell, at length, in detail, and one is almost tempted to say, with relish, on the guilt and misery that await Maria Rushworth, Henry Crawford, Mrs. Norris, and others. Jane Austen is one of the great portrayers of guilt, to be ranked along with Sophocles and Dostoevsky—guilt and its consequences in the way of misery; guilt and its redemption by remorse, self-examination, the acquisition of new insight, expiation. I can think of few English novelists in whose works the word itself occurs more frequently, except her mentor, Richardson. There are no finer self-recognition scenes in literature than those of Marianne Dashwood and Elizabeth Bennet—"How despicably have I acted! I, who have prided myself on my discernment! I, who have valued myself on my abilities! who have often disdained the generous candour of my sister, and gratified my vanity in useless or blameable distrust. How humiliating is this discovery! yet, how just a humiliation! . . . Till this moment I never knew myself" (*PP*, 208)—and, above all, that of Emma Woodhouse, which continues through several chapters, and stages of increasing intensity:

> Never had she felt so agitated, mortified, grieved, at any circumstance in her life. She was most forcibly struck. The truth of his representation there was no denying. She felt it at her heart. How could she have been so brutal, so cruel to Miss Bates! . . . Time did not compose her. As she reflected more, she seemed but to feel it more. She never had been so depressed. . . . Emma felt the tears running down her cheeks almost all the way home, without being at any trouble to check them, extraordinary as they were. (*E*, 376)
>
> "O God! that I had never seen her!"
>
> The rest of the day, the following night, were hardly enough for her thoughts. She was bewildered amidst the confusion of all that had rushed on her within the last few hours. Every moment had brought a fresh surprise; and every surprise must be matter of humiliation to her. How to understand it all! How to understand the deceptions she had been thus practising on herself, and living under! The blunders, the blindness of her own head and heart! She sat still, she walked about, she tried her own room, she tried the shrubbery—in every place, every posture, she perceived that she had acted most weakly; that she had been imposed on by others in a most mortifying degree; that she had been imposing on herself in a degree yet more mortifying; that she was wretched, and should probably find this day but the beginning of wretchedness.
>
> To understand, thoroughly understand her own heart, was the first endeavour. (411-412)

To reinforce the effect, Jane Austen even introduces one of her rare but always brilliant and significant natural descriptions: "The evening of this day was very long and melancholy at Hartfield. The weather added what it could of gloom. A cold stormy rain set in, and nothing of July appeared but in the trees and shrubs, which the wind was despoiling, and the length of the day, which only made such cruel sights the longer visible" (421). Few other pens have dwelt so long and so convincingly on guilt and misery as Jane Austen's. If the literal-minded critic asks in bewilderment,

"Why then does she confuse us by making the statement she does at the end of *Mansfield Park*?" Jane Austen's reply might only be to repeat sardonically her parody of Scott. "I do not write for such dull elves/As have not a great deal of ingenuity themselves" (*Letters*, 298).

III

"I could no more write a romance than an epic poem."[9] Exactly; Jane Austen's interest was in writing *novels*, as we now use the term, a term which was a relatively new one in her day—and the thing itself was not much older. Criticism of the novel, too, is still a young, immature business; one thinks of criticism of poetry and the drama, which, like those literary forms, goes back more than two millennia to Plato and Aristotle and during its long existence has managed to clarify at least some elementary causes of confusion for those who deal with these genres. Not so with criticism of the novel, which still seems to find some difficulty in distinguishing it from those two forms which Jane Austen so firmly renounces. There is a rather vague period of transition between the long prose romances of the Middle Ages, the Renaissance, and the seventeenth century—Heliodorus, Malory, La Calprenède—and the novel, a transition in which such works of fiction as those of Madame de Lafayette and Defoe and Mrs. Heywood (an unjustly neglected writer) show some characteristics of both forms.

But the break clearly comes with Richardson, and the distinction has never been better expounded than by Samuel Johnson, writing soon after *Clarissa* was published:

> The works of fiction with which the present generation seems more particularly delighted are such as exhibit life in its true state, diversified only by accidents that daily happen in the world, and influenced by passions and qualities which are really to be found in conversing with mankind. . . .

> Its province is to bring about natural events by easy means: it is therefore precluded from the machines and expedients of the heroic romance, and can neither employ giants to snatch away a lady from the nuptial rites, nor knights to bring her back from captivity; it can neither bewilder its personages in deserts, nor lodge them in imaginary castles. . . . All the fictions of the last age will vanish if you deprive them of a hermit and a wood, a battle and a shipwreck. . . . The task of our present writers is very different; it requires . . . that experience which can never be attained by solitary diligence, but must arise from general converse, and accurate observation, of the living world. Their performances have . . . little indulgence, and therefore more difficulty. They are engaged in portraits of which everyone knows the original, and can detect any deviation from exactness of resemblance.[10]

The appeal to the reader of the novel, so defined, comes not from "wonder"—the unfamiliar, the unexpected, the improbable—but from the familiar—from "the shock of recognition." The characters are not giants and wizards and spectres, gallant knights and beautiful princesses, but individuals with whom the reader can, as we say, "identify"—people of much the same social and economic and cultural background as the reader, or at least within a cultural spectrum with which the reader has had some direct contact; the scene not far away lands and distant times, but here and now.

The psychological rationale behind this is expounded in another *Rambler* essay a little later. Johnson is here talking primarily of biography and emphasizing its superiority to history as it was then written, but what he says applies equally to the superiority of the novel over the romance:

> All joy or sorrow for the happiness or calamities of others is produced by an act of the imagination, that realizes the event [makes it real], however fictitious, or approximates it [brings it close], however remote, by placing us, for a time, in the condition of him whose fortune we contem-

> plate; so that we feel while the deception lasts, whatever motions [emotions] would be excited by the same good or evil happening to ourselves.
>
> Our passions are therefore more strongly moved, in proportion as we can more readily adopt the pains or pleasures proposed to our minds, by recognizing them as once our own, or considering them as naturally incident to our state of life. It is not easy for the most artful writer to give us an interest in happiness or misery which we think ourselves never likely to feel, and with which we have never yet been made acquainted.[11]

Thus "the general and rapid narratives of history," with "the downfall of kingdoms, and revolutions of empires," are "read with great tranquility." No one can now get really much worked up about Alexander the Great's ups and downs during his conquest of Persia 2,200 years ago—unless, like Mary Renault, one transforms Alexander into a clever and neurotic young man of the twentieth century, in which case there seems little point in calling him "Alexander" and transporting him back to the third century B.C. But one can still get worked up about Clarissa Harlowe, who could be the girl next door, or at least in the next suburb—the one individual with integrity and a capacity for emotion in a grasping and unscrupulous determinedly upward-mobile family, who have no other values than the acquisition of more wealth and social status and will let nothing stand in their way, certainly not their youngest daughter's whims about love and respect as the basis for a marriage—a girl who, in a desperate attempt at escape, falls victim to a charismatic psychopath.

Hence, Johnson continues, the most effective biography—and, by extension, novel—is not that which deals with great public figures, but with the ordinary individual. "I have often thought that there has rarely passed a life of which a judicious and faithful narrative would not be useful"—a modern variant is the saying that every person has at least one novel in him, if he could write the story of his own life accurately and without concealment.

"It is frequently objected to relations of particular lives," Johnson continues, "that they are not distinguished by any striking or wonderful vicissitudes"—and is not this what the complaint about Jane Austen's "limitations" in the end boils down to? "The scholar who passed his life among his books, the merchant who conducted only his own affairs, the priest whose sphere of action was not extended beyond that of his duty, are considered as no proper objects of public regard, however they might have excelled in their several stations, whatever might have been their learning, integrity, and piety. . . . But," says Johnson in a magnificent retort to such objectors that deserves to be printed in italics, "*this notion arises from false measures of excellence and dignity*."[12] The mental anguish of an Emma Woodhouse, its causes and its cure, are quite as important in the sum total of things, quite as worthy of the attention and emotion of the intelligent adult reader, as the melodramatic rantings of Shakespeare's Cleopatra or the monumental swivings of some macho hero of Norman Mailer or Henry Miller or the later Hemingway.

These remarks of Johnson, and the kind of fiction writing they are based on, mark, I think, a real revolution in the history of literature, a break with the past which has been dimly recognized by literary historians but not sufficiently stressed, and I am arguing that the charge of limitation against Jane Austen is an obsolete holdover from pre-Johnsonian notions of the nature of fiction. There are two parts to Johnson's thesis. The first is that the effectiveness of literature comes from its empathetic power: its ability to "place us, for a time, in the condition of him whose fortune we contemplate; so that we feel, while the deception lasts"—one recalls Coleridge's "willing suspension of disbelief"—"whatever emotions would be excited by the same good or evil happening to ourselves." I do not know whether the concept of "identification" or "empathy" between the reader and those about whom he reads was ever formulated earlier; but if so, it has never been so well expressed, and it is basic to Johnson's view of literature, which instructs by pleasing. I once tried to make this phrase more intelligible to the modern student by paraphrasing it in modern jargon: "By involving the reader emotionally, it effects desirable changes in his nervous system."

No doubt such involvement, such empathy, took place with the earlier romance: the reader, or listener, did imagine himself the knight errant of the tale and did experience vicariously his fear when he encountered the dragon and his joy when he slew it and rescued the beautiful maiden. But such emotions, Johnson feels, are on a pretty elementary level, so trivial and transitory that they do not seriously affect the reader's attitude toward life—unless, of course, he is psychotic, like Don Quixote, and the many imitations of him so popular in England in the next century: Arabella, the "female Quixote"; Geoffrey Wildgoose, the "spiritual Quixote"; Sir Lancelot Greaves, Sir Hudibras, and so on. (Interesting that, just at the time the realistic novel was emerging, there should have been this spate of satires on those whose addled brains responded so vigorously to the chivalric romances.) They are appropriate fodder for children and primitive peoples—indeed, Johnson used to relax his mind by reading them occasionally, as a modern scholar might read detective fiction or watch Lord Peter Wimsey on television. But they are not serious reading for mature and civilized men and women: "Why this wild strain of imagination found reception so long, in polite and learned ages, it is not easy to conceive."[13] And it does seem odd that La Calprenède and Racine should have been contemporaries.

Second, if this condition for serious literature is accepted, it follows that the bulk of the characters in a work of fiction must be socially and culturally close enough to its readers as to facilitate such empathy. A great genius like Shakespeare (or Racine) may be able to overcome the handicap that his characters belong to a class or culture or time remote from that of the readers. But Shakespeares are rare:

> Other dramatists can only gain attention by hyperbolical or aggravated characters, by fabulous and unexampled excellence or depravity, as the writers of barbarous romances invigorated the reader by a giant and a dwarf; and he that should form his expectations of human affairs from the play, or from the tale, would be equally deceived. Shakespeare has no heroes; his scenes are occupied only by men, who act and speak as the reader thinks that he should himself have spoken or acted on the same occasion. . . . Shakespeare approximates the remote, and familiarizes the wonderful; the event which he represents will not happen, but if it were possible, its effects would be probably such as he has assigned.[14]

Johnson feels that Shakespeare was handicapped by the stage conventions of his time and the taste of its audiences, "a people newly awakened to literary curiosity." "A play which imitated only the common occurrences of the world," he writes, "would, upon the admirers of *Palmerin* and *Guy of Warwick*, have made little impression; he that wrote for such an audience was under the necessity of looking round for strange events and fabulous transactions."[15] Shakespeare's genius, that is to say, would have shown to even greater advantage had he, like Richardson, set the scene of *Hamlet* and *Lear* in contemporary England and made the characters members of his own middle class; and who is to say that Johnson was wrong?

This brings us to matters of sociology and social history, and to Arnold Kettle's charge—and that of many others—of "social limitation" against Jane Austen. It might be argued that Johnson's manifesto, far from limiting, rather has a broadening effect: it is a manifesto of the "rising middle class," who are now the principal audience for literature and whose importance must be recognized in it. Of course, as historians point out, the middle class had been rising for a long time, and obviously there were many of them around in Shakespeare's day. Yet it is hard not to wonder, along with Johnson, at how slowly its recognition in literature took place. In Shakespeare and his contemporary playwrights, as in Homer and Aeschylus and Seneca before them, there are basically only two social classes of characters, the "high," who constitute the heroes and heroines and villains, and the "clowns," humble messengers and servants, often figures of fun; there cannot have been too much "identification" by those of Shakespeare's audience who had a background similar to his own. At least this is true of the tragedies and the histories (with the conspicuous exception of I and II *Henry IV* and *Henry V*). In many of the comedies the leading characters are not quite so highborn; they may be from the merchant class, like the Antipholuses of the *Comedy of Errors* and Antonio and Bassanio of *The Merchant of Venice*. And this fact calls attention to the significance of Johnson's attempt to define the novel: "This kind of writing may be termed not improperly the comedy of romance, and is to be conducted nearly by the rules of comic poetry"[16]—that is, by the conventions formulated by Aristotle on the basis of the comic drama of the Greeks and later by Romans such as Plautus, from whom the *Comedy of Errors* is taken. "Tragedy is an imitation of persons who are above the common level," says Aristotle, and "comedy is an imitation of characters of a lower type." The term, he thinks, comes from the Doric *komai*, villages: "comedians were so named . . . because they wandered from village to village, being excluded contemptuously from the city."[17]

It still bothered Johnson's contemporaries and many after them when Richardson published serious, even tragic stories in which members of the middle class—even somewhere between "lower middle" and "working" class, like Pamela Andrews—were the central figures and readers were asked to take their emotions seriously. There was a great deal of snobbery among professional writers in the eighteenth and nineteenth centuries, many of whom suffered an acute sense of inferiority at doing something so "low" as to write for money. Fielding, an Old Etonian and the cousin of an earl, seemed particularly afraid of being thought déclassé, and to feel outraged at a story in which a humble servant girl rises to the status of "lady." The suggestion that Pamela has sincere and deep emotions worthy of serious attention by a reader of the upper classes infuriates him, and he has to degrade her, as Shamela, to the time-honored role of her class in fiction as comic butt, or conniving and amoral soubrette. In *Joseph Andrews* she becomes "Mrs. Booby" (and, in time, presumably "Lady Booby"); and the fun at the beginning of the book comes from what Fielding thinks the comic incongruity of Lady Booby senior making eyes at Pamela's humble footman brother—such crossing of class-lines is reprehensible, and must be put down with scathing satire. (But what happens later in the book, and in *Amelia*, is another matter. It is almost as though Fielding, who had come to scoff at Richardson, remained to pray.)

Even in Scott and Dickens and beyond, much remains of the old dichotomy between the genteel central figures of the action—those boring, upright heroes and heroines of Scott, the noble and wooden Agnes Wickfield and Lucie Manette and Harry Maylie and Rose Fleming—and the comic or quaint or pathetic low appendages of the central plot. Although the other characters with whom Oliver Twist associates in the first ten years of his life speak several amusing varieties of substandard English, concocted with all Dickens's verbal skill, Oliver, born and bred in the workhouse, from the first miraculously speaks nothing but the purest, most grammatical BBC English. The experienced reader is thus able to foresee from the beginning that Oliver, unlike Noah Claypole and the Artful Dodger, will turn out in the end to be the long-lost child of gentlefolk, his "stain of illegitimacy," unlike Harriet Smith's, thoroughly "bleached" by inherited wealth and position.

IV

Jane Austen declared her inability, or unwillingness, to write romance or epic. It is worth noting that, while Johnson thought the novel to be related to comic *drama*, Fielding preferred to think of it as comic *epic*. There are crucial differences between the two conceptions. In the classical literature from which both writers drew their terms, there *is* comic drama, that of Aristophanes, Plautus, and the rest, in which, as we have seen, the characters are of a "lower" type than the characters of tragedy, who are "above the common level." "Lower," not "low," it should be noted, meaning that they may be *of* the common level, or middle class, as indeed most of the central characters in Aristophanes and Plautus and Terence may be described. On the other hand, there is no such thing in classical literature as Fielding's "comic epic." The classical epic of Homer and Virgil eschews the comic—it is grimly serious, even pompous—and it equally eschews any but characters "above the common level": its announced purpose is to celebrate a hero and his almost equally heroic companions and their heroic actions. Gods themselves enter the action, ranging themselves for or against the hero and his proposed feats of heroism. The epic is, indeed, the ancestor of the romance, the early romances, about Alexander and Charlemagne and Arthur, clearly taking their inspiration from watered-down Homer and Virgil and Statius. Jane Austen did well to lump them together as what she wanted to avoid.

Fielding's new "comic epic," as he describes it in the preface to *Joseph Andrews*,[18] is not quite the same as the popular "mock epic" of Boileau and Pope. Still, Fielding makes it clear that it may involve ridicule and "burlesque . . . as in the description of the battles, and some other places," so that some at least of the comedy comes from the writer's deliberately putting down, making fun of, the genre he is ostensibly working in, a technique which adds peculiar difficulties to the writer's task. It differs from the true epic by, among other things, "introducing persons of inferior rank, and consequently [sic!—here speaks the Old Etonian] of inferior manners." Nevertheless to have the semblance of an epic, the fiction of its centering on a hero must be kept up (both

Joseph Andrews and Tom Jones, like Oliver Twist, turn out in the end to be "long-lost sons" of genteel parentage). And it retains several of the traditional structural elements of the classical epic, notably the "episode"—the long digression, the interpolated tale—of which Fielding, Scott, Dickens, and others were so fond; the intrusive narrator, who begins the work with an address to his readers setting forth his purpose and from time to time editorializes on what he has been narrating ("Tantae molis erat Romanam condere gentem"); the general impression of bigness, not to say inflation—"differing from comedy [comic drama] as the serious epic from tragedy: its action being more extended and comprehensive; containing a much larger circle of incidents, and introducing a greater variety of characters."

It is perhaps ironic that Fielding, who began his career as a dramatist—though, let us face it, not a very good dramatist, except when he is writing burlesque of high tragedy like *Tom Thumb*—should have taken the epic as his model when beginning to write prose fiction. Jane Austen did not entirely eschew some of the epic devices: there is the occasional intervention by the narrator, though given her penchant for irony, it can be dangerous to take these too seriously. (In spite of its obvious satire on the values of Mrs. Bennet and her like, it is to be feared that critics like Arnold Kettle really think that the statement "it is a truth universally acknowledged that a single man in possession of a good fortune must be in want of a wife" somehow or other represents Jane Austen's view.) I should like to argue, however, that Jane Austen's ideal for the novel, like Richardson's before her, is not the epic but the drama and that this fact accounts for some very important distinctions that occur in the history of the novel, between the Richardson-Jane Austen-Henry James tradition on the one hand and the Fielding-Scott-Dickens tradition on the other.

Jane Austen wrote considerable (comic) drama in her teens. Drama is, or should be, neat, compact, tightly structured; epic (and its offspring the romance and the picaresque) sprawls. Drama has a limited cast of characters, all in some way interrelated; epic, stretching over long periods of time and areas of space, has no limit on the number of incidental characters who may be introduced without warning, play their part in the action, and are then abandoned and forgotten, as the hero and his companions journey on their way. Epic is a *tale*, a telling (Greek *epos*, a word; "that which is spoken, uttered in words, a speech, tale"),[19] narrated by a teller, who is at liberty to intrude and comment whenever he feels like it, or to interrupt his main narrative at any time to insert another tale that comes to his mind. Drama is a continuous *action* (*drao*, I do, I act), watched by an audience with no intermediary between it and the actors. The milieu of the Fieldingesque novel is that of villagers gathered around a fire in the evening, while the wandering bard recites, with gestures and commentary, the deeds of faraway heroes in faraway lands and times (history in fact, which Johnson thought inferior to biography). The setting of the Jane Austen novel is the brightly lit stage of the Mansfield Park theatre, the audience, with no intervening commentator, watching Elizabeth and Darcy and Miss Bingley and Bingley and Mr. and Mrs. Hurst act and recite the brilliant dialogue of the scenes in the Netherfield drawing room (chapters 8 to 11 of *Pride and Prejudice*, which could be staged without any adaptation—the dialogue, the stage directions, the instructions to the actors about motivation and expression are all there—as could many other parts of Jane Austen's novels).

"Dramatize, dramatize, dramatize" was Henry James's advice to the novelist, and he tried to do so himself. So did Jane Austen, whose distaste for interpolated moral sermons and digressive ghost and other stories in the novels of her contemporaries thus becomes understandable. So did her teacher Richardson. The epistolary form, without even an impersonal, faceless narrator to intervene between the reader and the words of the actors, is the purest form of dramatization in the novel. (Theatrical producers have only recently become aware of the effectiveness of a "play" that is simply the reading on a stage of both sides of a correspondence, such as that between Bernard Shaw and Mrs. Pat Campbell.) Jane Austen wrote much, and well, in the epistolary novel-form in her youth.[20] It had gone out of fashion by the time she was ready to publish. Nevertheless in her mature novels one still feels the *dramatic* urge to present action directly and vividly to the reader, allowing *him* to observe and make up his mind about what is going on, and refusing to take the easy way out by *telling* him what to think. As Johnson said, the art of the modern novelist involves "more difficulty" than that of the writer of romance.

This is to oversimplify, of course. There are Fieldingesque passages of straightforward editorializing in Jane Austen, though, with her skill at perfect deadpan irony, it is often harder than with Fielding to tell what she means; there are brilliant Austenian dramatic scenes in Fielding. The answer to the problem of the technique of novel-writing remains a choice among a number of unsatisfactory compromises: Fielding's method of using the "personal" narrator will always entail his distasteful intervention between the characters of the novel and the reader; the "omniscient" impersonal narrator the question, "How does this mysterious individual come to know what is going on in the minds and feelings of the characters?"; any first-person narration, the question of how this monologue or journal or autobiography came to be set down in the first place; the "stream of consciousness" the question of whether or not one's "consciousness" ever verbalizes so glibly; the epistolary technique, praiseworthy though it is in giving us, with dramatic directness, the unmediated words of the characters, the question, so often raised with *Pamela* and *Clarissa*, of how the characters managed to find the time and opportunity, among their many other hectic occupations, to pen such frequent lengthy epistles. But I still think that much in the history of the novel is explained by the theory of its double origin—on the one hand, from the epic and romance, with their tendency to sprawl, to digress, to see bigness as a virtue in itself, to deal with large historical events, to hanker after deeds and individuals on a "heroic" scale, to describe things in black and white, exaggerating the goodness of the hero and the badness of the villains; and on the other hand, from the drama, in particular the comic drama, with its neatness and compactness, its preference for "ordinary," easily recognizable characters, its directness of presentation of their words and actions, its unwillingness to intrude with sermonizing and philosophizing, its preference for saying to the reader, in effect, "That's how it was; make up your own mind about it." To this "dramatic" tradition, Jane Austen and Richardson and Flaubert and Henry James are clearly closer than are Fielding and Scott and Dickens.

V

What I am saying, then, is that Jane Austen's alleged limitations are a *necessary* ingredient of her dramatic, as opposed to epic, technique of novel-writing—the technique where, in my opinion, as in James's, the true genius of the novel lies.[21] How one's heart sinks when one encounters the term *epic* in the advertising for the latest best-seller—James Michener's epics about Hawaii and Colorado (his latest book, one gathers, starts virtually with the Creation and brings one laboriously up through the magma, the dinosaurs, the mound builders, the early white settlers, the Civil War, etc., etc., to 1974); Irving Stone's massive "heroic" works about Michelangelo and Freud; Harold Robbins; the later Edna Ferber; *et hoc genus omne.* "Epic" motion-pictures "with a cast of thousands" are made out of them, epic sums of money accrue to those creating them, and in two years they are forgotten, never to be revived or reread. They rise, they shine, evaporate, and fall. If Austenian limitation is a fault, what then is the converse, which presumably must be excellence? In what sort of work do we get the most laudable *lack* of limitation, the largest quota of death, sex, hunger, war, guilt, and God, to cite Dorothy Van Ghent's desiderata? I mentioned James Jones; another, even better, nominee, containing vast quantities of all these (with the exception, of course, of God), is the interminable Lanny Budd series by the late Upton Sinclair, a minutely detailed, inaccurate, and tendentious history of the first half of the twentieth century as seen through the eyes of Sinclair's wooden protagonist. What ever happened to this epic masterpiece? It seems to have sunk without trace and is not likely to resurface.

The fact is that hankering after the "epic" novel has brought artistic (if not monetary) disaster to innumerable promising younger novelists. Edna Ferber's first success *So Big* (ironic title), a rather charming and thoughtful story about a young and vivacious school teacher of the 1890s, who marries a stolid market gardener and spends the rest of her life growing tomatoes on a small farm on the outskirts of Chicago, might have had some appeal for Jane Austen. But presently we get into something a little bigger, life on a showboat up and down the Mississippi, with a sprinkling of "social consciousness"; and eventually we have "epics" dealing with the history and sociology of Texas and Alaska. Michener's first book, *Tales of the South Pacific*, is a somewhat inflated but fairly readable and convincing series of vignettes of life during World War II in various Pacific islands. What the bitch goddess "epic" wrought there, we know. Perhaps the most lamentable disaster of the century was Hemingway, who, when writing within his "limitations," in his early short stories and his first novel, *The Sun Also Rises*—its cast of characters, half a dozen or so, is at least as limited a social and cultural group as any in Jane Austen—displayed the makings of a great novelist. But with his next—and more popular—effort, *A Farewell to Arms*, we get a broader "scope," with scenes from the Great War; and after that comes an "epic" of the Spanish Civil War (with lots of social and political "philosophizing," such as Arnold Kettle would approve of). And then—. One could go on indefinitely.

Am I being unfair in selecting such hack "epics" to contrast with Jane Austen? Are there not novels which transcend such limitations as hers and, through their authors' ability to handle more "strong, manly, spirited" topics, "full of variety and glow," such as those listed by Dorothy Van Ghent, rank higher as masterpieces than hers? For reasons of space, let us consider just one of those topics, war. Here, I'm afraid, we can't help touching incidentally on an unpleasant matter. Is there not a good deal of machismo—our old friend "male chauvinism"—built into the critical values that would downgrade Jane Austen's novels because of their "limitations" and exalt, say, Hemingway's instead?[22] Only males can play the role of epic hero, can lead an assault against Troy, found Rome, battle Poseidon for ten years: thus epics are ipso facto off limits for women writers, who by definition can have had none of these experiences—indeed the women in Homer and Virgil, like Dido and Circe, generally serve as obstacles to the men in accomplishing their heroic tasks; except, of course, good old Penelope, the eternal suburban housewife, who knows that woman's place is in the home. When it comes to the Napoleonic War, Jane Austen is in a double bind. She is severely criticized for the limitations that make her unable to write about it. You imagine what would have happened had she gone up to the recruiting office in Brighton Camp and said, "I am a novelist. It is necessary for me to acquire some military experience in order to correct my novelistic limitations. I'd like to sign up as a private in the Buffs." As a woman, of course, she had no chance of getting anywhere near the fighting, even as an ambulance-driver, like Hemingway—no more than she had of getting into Winchester College and Oxford University. Therefore Hemingway, laudably free from such limitations, becomes a greater novelist than Jane Austen. Too bad, Miss Austen, but that's the way the cookie crumbles. I was sorry to find my former colleague, the late Dorothy Van Ghent, usually too astute to be taken in by such things, listing the exclusively male occupation of war as one of the ingredients of the "unlimited" novel. At least it can be argued that women as well as men can know something about death, hunger, sex, guilt, and God, though I have the uneasy feeling that many critics, perhaps even Professor Van Ghent, have unconsciously assumed that men, somehow or other, know them *better*.

To get on with the Napoleonic War. There are a number of admittedly great novels which do mention it: *Vanity Fair*, *La Chartreuse de Parme*, *War and Peace*. But just what role does the Battle of Waterloo play in *Vanity Fair*? We see some of the fringes of it: the Duchess of Richmond's ball, the only interest of which in the novel is that it provides the setting for George Osborne's attempt at adultery with Becky Sharpe; the departure of the British troops from Brussels, which allows us to observe the various ways in which Becky, Jos, and Mrs. O'Dowd cope with an emergency. Of the battle itself we have one short, dull paragraph of editorializing and one perfunctory paragraph of narrative—the fact is that Jane Austen in *Persuasion* tells us *more* about naval action in the Napoleonic War than Thackeray does about military—and then the magnificent conclusion, which is the main justification for bringing in the Battle of Waterloo at all: "No more firing was heard at Brussels—the pursuit rolled miles away. Darkness came down on the field and city, and Amelia was praying for George, who was lying on his face, dead, with a bullet through his heart." Moving; but what, really, does the Battle of Waterloo have to do with it? If George had been killed by an accidental discharge of a gun during a shooting party at Lord Steyne's country seat—or breaking his neck on the Cobb at Lyme—it would have served the purposes of the novel just as well.

There is rather more narrative of military action in *La Chartreuse*, but not much. Fabrice gets caught up in it by accident, greatly to his bewilderment; the whole point of the incident (which really occupies a very small place in the novel) is that it is pointless, "absurd." There *is* considerable (rather boring) editorializing in *War and Peace* and a considerable amount of detailed military history. But the thesis of the editorializing is much the same as Stendhal's—war is not the portentous, superlative expression of the human mind and will that people (say, critics of Jane Austen's limitations) seem to think; it is blind, confused, absurd; and those who, like Napoleon, believe they are controlling it are deceiving themselves. In the descriptions of action, Napoleon shrinks to a comic figure: it is the small individuals, the captain and gunners of a rear-guard artillery battery, Andrei and Pierre wrestling with their intimate spiritual problems (while Emma Woodhouse, back at Hartfield, was wrestling with hers—does the geographical setting make that much difference?) that are interesting and important. Much more space in the novel is devoted to peace than to war, and it is the thoughts and feelings of the handful of the Russian nobility—what deplorable "class limitation"!—that the novel deals with that we remember and are intended to remember, not Napoleon's and Kutuzov's tactics at Borodino. I should like to mention one other war novel that I admire. Evelyn Waugh's fine trilogy of the Second World War. Again, like Tolstoy, it is not the war as such that interests Waugh—the war itself, and its "leaders," are as absurd in Waugh's book as in Tolstoy's. There is a section in it about the British evacuation of Crete that is as fine and as knowledgeable a description of a military operation as any in Tolstoy; but, as in Tolstoy, it is a series of disconnected fragmentary episodes, seen through the eyes of the individuals who experience them. What goes on in the minds and feelings of human beings at Borodino and Crete is no more, and no less, important than what goes on in them at Hartfield and Longbourn. "We are all prompted by the same motives, all deceived by the same fallacies, all animated by hope, obstructed by danger, entangled by desire, and seduced by pleasure":[23] it is the novelist's task to make us, through the accuracy of his observation of our fellow human beings and his skill in presenting them convincingly, respond as his characters do to such circumstances. The setting, in time and place, is of no importance in itself, nor are the particular incidents which give rise to the danger, the desire, and the rest. The only "limitation" of the novelist that matters is that of his ability to observe accurately and present effectively.

Throughout the last book of Waugh's trilogy runs, like a refrain, a comment made by one of the characters on the moral issues raised by the war, a comment which might be taken to heart by critics of the novel—"Quantitative judgments don't apply." The quantity of characters, the quantity of incident, the quantity of violence, the quantity of sexual couplings, the quantity of historical information, the quantity of social and political and philosophical sermonizing in a novel is perfectly irrelevant to its artistic effectiveness. Even by quantitative criteria, however, Jane Austen's novels are no more limited than Tolstoy's or James's, and much less limited than Hemingway's later ones. The social, cultural, and psychological range of the characters, with vulgarians low in the social scale like Mr. Price and Lucy Steele and high in it like Lady Catherine and Sir Walter Elliot, with crooks like Wickham and weaklings like Willoughby, with comic (and pathetic) idiots like Mr. Collins and Mr. Elton, with sex-kittens like Lydia Bennet and neurotic adulteresses like Maria Rushworth, with bluff and attractive extroverts like Admiral and Mrs. Croft, with menaces like General Tilney and Mr. and Mrs. John Dashwood—one could go on for a long time, and this is only to mention some of the minor characters, without touching on the complex major ones—is quite as varied in Tolstoy's small circle of noble Russian families or James's of international socialites or Joyce's of lower middleclass Dubliners: more varied than the boring handful of stereotypes in the later Hemingway and other Nobel Prize winners. There is plenty of sex in them—to repeat, illicit sex is the hinge on which the plot turns in *Pride and Prejudice* and *Mansfield Park*, and it would be naive to think that sex does not form a good deal of the attraction of Marianne to Willoughby or of Emma to Frank Churchill. The war is there, all right: it is essential to the plot of *Persuasion* and to that of *Pride and Prejudice*—those who remember from World War II the effect on adolescent girls of the proximity of a great military camp such as that at Brighton, or even a small detachment of soldiers, as in Meryton, will recognize the electricity in the air that affects Lydia and Kitty. There is much keen and realistic observation of the facts of economics—even the possibility of "hunger," or at least squalor, in the lives of Jane Fairfax and Fanny Price and Mrs. Smith. The middleclass milieu of Jane Austen's characters is not really too distant from that of most of her middleclass American readers even today—money and sex and marriage and social climbing are still problems for them; *less* distant, surely, than that of Tolstoy's or James's or Joyce's characters; certainly much less distant than Dickens's. If "contiguity with modern interests," as Dorothy Van Ghent puts it, is the chief desideratum in a novel—and I believe, with Johnson, that it is—it is there. But that contiguity comes not from the fact that Jane Austen and her people are quite as involved as twentieth-century readers with "death, sex, hunger, war, guilt, God"—though they are—but from the qualities which Ezra Pound attributed to Joyce's *Ulysses* and Eliot's *Prufrock:* "James Joyce has written the best novel of a decade, and perhaps the best criticism of it has come from a Belgian who said, 'All this is as true of my country as of Ireland.' Eliot has a like ubiquity of application. Art does not avoid universals, it strikes at them the harder in that it strikes through particularities. . . . His men in shirt-sleeves and his society ladies are not a local manifestation: they are the stuff of our modern world, and true of more countries than one."[24] What Jane Austen narrates is as true of twentieth-century America as of nineteenth-century Hartfield; her characters are the stuff of our modern world, and true of more countries than one.

NOTES

1. Such as G. K. Chesterton: "She was naturally exuberant. Her power came as all power comes, from the direction and control of exuberance. But there is the presence and pressure of that vitality behind her thousand trivialities; she could have been extravagant if she liked. She was the very reverse of a starched or a starved spinster; she could have been a buffoon like the Wife of Bath if she chose" (*Love and Friendship* [New York: Frederick A. Stokes, 1922], p. xv).

2. *An Introduction to the English Novel* (New York: Harper, 1960), 1:98-99.

3. *The English Novel: A Panorama* (Boston: Houghton Mifflin, 1960), pp. 189-190.

4. *The English Novel: Form and Function* (New York: Harper, 1953), p. 99.

5. In quotations from Jane Austen and Samuel Johnson, I have modernized spelling and punctuation.

6. One wonders whether it was Jane Austen's publishers or her family who were responsible for the deletion from the second edition of *Sense and Sensibility* ("in the interests of propriety": R. W. Chapman) of the last sentence in the following passage:

> "And who is Miss Williams?" asked Marianne.
>
> ". . . She is a relation of the Colonel's, my dear; a very near relation. We will not say how near, for fear of shocking the young ladies." Then lowering her voice a little, she said to Elinor [aged nineteen], "She is his natural daughter." . . .
>
> Lady Middleton's delicacy was shocked; and in order to banish so improper a subject as the mention of a natural daughter, she actually took the trouble of saying something about the weather (*SS*, xiv, 66, 384).

7. Her memory is good: Isabella wrote out the story, and Lovell read it aloud. The congratulations to Isabella at the end make it sound as though she were the reader.

8. One wonders whether the caption on the title page of Jane Austen's first published work, "By a Lady," is not rather a challenge

than an expression of modesty. It seems to have confused whoever wrote the advertisements for it: "A new novel by Lady ——" and "Interesting Novel by Lady A——" (*SS*, xiii).

9. It is interesting that, though the terms do not appear on the title pages, Jane Austen's last volume was advertised as "Northanger Abbey, a Romance; and Persuasion, a Novel" (*NA* and *P*, xiii).

10. *Rambler*, no. 4, *Works* (New Haven: Yale University Press, 1958-), 3:19-20.

11. *Rambler*, no. 60, *Works*, 3:318-319.

12. Ibid., p. 320.

13. *Rambler*, no. 4, *Works*, 3:20.

14. "Preface to Shakespeare," *Works*, 7:64-65.

15. Ibid., p. 82.

16. *Rambler*, no. 4, *Works*, 3:19.

17. *Poetics*, tr. S. H. Butcher, sec. XV, V, III (in *Plato to Alexander Pope: Backgrounds of Modern Criticism*, ed. Walter Sutton [New York: Odyssey, 1966]).

18. *Works* (Middletown, Conn.: Wesleyan University Press, 1967-), 1:3-11.

19. Liddell and Scott, *Greek-English Lexicon*, abr. (New York: American Book Co., n.d.).

20. *Sense and Sensibility* was originally "written in the form of letters, and was read aloud"—no doubt with various members of the Austen family assuming the roles of the various correspondents (*SS*, xiii).

21. If I am right in tracing a double origin of the modern novel from the epic (Fielding) and the drama (Johnson), James and the rest, in preferring the "dramatic" novel, seem to have Aristotle on their side. The *Poetics* ends with a comparative evaluation of epic and tragedy (it is the formal elements of tragedy that are discussed, elements found in comic as well as tragic drama): "[Tragedy] has vividness of impression in reading as well as in representation. Moreover, the art attains its end within narrower limits, for the concentrated effect is more pleasurable than one which is spread over a long time and so diluted. . . . The epic imitation has less unity, as is shown by this, that any epic poem will furnish subjects for several tragedies [cf. the interpolated story of the Hartz Demon]. Thus, if the story adopted by the poet has a strict unity, it must either be concisely told and appear truncated; or, if it conform to

the epic canon of length, it must seem weak and watery. . . . If, then, tragedy is superior to epic poetry in all these respects . . . it plainly follows that tragedy is the higher art, as attaining its end more perfectly" (tr. Butcher, sec. XXVI).

22. "For a long time . . . the Fielding-Scott-Dickens fanciers controlled criticism of the novel in England, defending their preferred authors, in more genteel times, as 'cleaner' than Richardson and his school, and, in less genteel days, as more 'vigorous.' Always they depreciated the strain that passes from Richardson to Jane Austen to George Eliot to Henry James as somehow too feminine and inward to be truly Anglo-Saxon": Leslie Fiedler, *Love and Death in the American Novel* (Cleveland: World, 1962), p. 42. The thesis that Fiedler goes on to develop—which seems to me an entirely accurate one—is that it is the main tradition of the American novel, from Fenimore Cooper, Melville, Mark Twain, to Hemingway and Faulkner, the tradition of a fictional world of "men without women" (except insofar as women are pliant sex-objects or else would-be castrators) that suffers from "limitation."

23. Johnson, *Rambler*, no. 60, *Works*, 3:320.

24. *Instigations* (New York: Boni and Liveright, 1920), p. 199; originally published in *Poetry* (1917).

THE CONTRIBUTORS

Robert Alan Donovan is professor of English at the State University of New York at Albany. He is the author of *The Shaping Vision: Imagination in the English Novel from Defoe to Dickens* and of numerous articles on eighteenth- and nineteenth-century English literature.

Alistair M. Duckworth is associate professor of English at the University of Florida and author of *The Improvement of the Estate: A Study of Jane Austen's Novels.*

Donald Greene is Leo S. Bing Professor of English at the University of Southern California. Among his books are *The Politics of Samuel Johnson*, *The Age of Exuberance*, and with James L. Clifford *Samuel Johnson: A Survey and Bibliography of Critical Studies.* He is co-editor of *Eighteenth-Century Studies* and first secretary of the American Society for Eighteenth-Century Studies.

Karl Kroeber is chairman of the Department of English and Comparative Literature at Columbia University. Among his recent publications are *Styles in Fictional Structure: The Art of Jane Austen, Charlotte Brontë, George Eliot;* and *Romantic Landscape Vision: Constable and Wordsworth.*

Juliet McMaster, associate professor of English at the University of Alberta, is the author of *Thackeray: The Major Novels* and of a number of articles on John Ford, Defoe, Sterne, Austen, Thackeray, Trollope, and James.

Norman Page, associate professor of English at the University of Alberta, has published *The Language of Jane Austen*, *Speech in the English Novel*, and *Wilkie Collins: The Critical Heritage*, as well as an edition of *Bleak House* and many articles on the nineteenth-century novel.

Joel Weinsheimer, assistant professor of English at Texas Tech University, has published several articles on Jane Austen and is co-editor (with Barry Roth) of *An Annotated Bibliography of Jane Austen Studies, 1952-1972* and (with Jeffrey Smitten) of *Studies in Burke and His Time*.

Joseph Wiesenfarth is associate professor of English at the University of Wisconsin at Madison. His first book on Henry James was followed by *The Errand of Form*, which addresses itself to critical problems in Jane Austen's novels.